201 Ways to Turn
Any Employee into
A Star Performer

201 Ways to Turn Any Employee into A Star Performer

Casey Fitts Hawley

McGraw-Hill
New York   Chicago   San Francisco   Lisbon   London
Madrid   Mexico City   Milan   New Delhi
San Juan   Seoul   Singapore   Sydney   Toronto

The McGraw·Hill Companies

1 2 3 4 5 6 7 8 9 0 DOC/DOC 0 9 8 7 6 5 4

ISBN 0-07-143370-8

McGraw-Hill books are available at special quantity discounts to use as premiums and sales promotions, or for use in corporate training programs. For more information, please write to the Director of Special Sales, McGraw-Hill Professional, Two Penn Plaza, New York, NY 10121-2298. Or contact your local bookstore.

 This book is printed on recycled, acid-free paper containing a minimum of 50% recycled, de-inked fiber.

Library of Congress Cataloging-in-Publication Data

Hawley, Casey Fitts.
    201 ways to turn any employee into a star performer / Casey Fitts Hawley.
        p. cm.
    Includes index.
    ISBN 0-07-143370-8 (alk. paper)
    1. Problem employees.   2. Employee motivation.   3. Performance—Management.   4. Super-vision of employees.   5. Personnel management.   I. Title: Two hundred one ways to turn any employee into a star performer.   II. Title: Two hundred and one ways to turn any employee into a star performer.   III. Title.

HF5549.5.E42H39   2003
658.3'124—dc22
                                               2004000403

To Zachary Katz and Houston Hawley, two men who have always been star performers. May you always be blessed and know the satisfaction of being "workmen worthy of your hire" (Matthew 10:10). And to Ruthe Cox, a professional who did all the things in this book perfectly, yet found time to be an inspiration and a friend to countless folks like me. How fortunate I have been to have her as a model for handling life's constant surprises.

Contents

1

An Introduction to Performance Issues

Performance management is an art, a science, and an ongoing study for top managers who get results. Influencing employees to alter their performance is the toughest but most valuable leadership challenge of all. *201 Ways to Turn Any Employee into a Star Performer* explores the best practices and most effective strategies for turning around performance problems. Some of the interventions apply to employees who have serious problems; even more apply to those who simply are not reaching the stellar level of performance that is possible for them. The return on an investment in performance management is high—it is worth the time and resources that it may cost. Everybody wins when performance goes up a notch: the department, the company, the manager, the customer, the stockholders, but most of all, the performer who experiences greater success. To understand how to deliver this type of success to your organization and your employees, you will need a foundational knowledge of performance issues in today's fast-paced work environment.

PERFORMANCE IMPROVEMENT IS HARDER TODAY

Improving performance just isn't as easy as it used to be. Why? For one reason, employees have already experienced every performance improvement program or philosophy out there: motivational programs, process improvement, gurus, consultants, PI, PM, TQM, and ISO 9000! "One person can improve only so much," today's employee says to him- or herself, "and I think I stretched beyond that limit a few years ago."

While employers continue to push for doing more with less, employees are saying, "We're at the zero point. There is nothing left to trim, give up, or reduce. We're already doing the job in less time and with fewer resources than it takes to perform."

And yet, managers are still being asked to get increased performance from an already overextended workforce. How can this be accomplished? *One employee at a time.*

IMPROVING PERFORMANCE ONE EMPLOYEE AT A TIME: 11 TRUISMS

You can improve an individual's performance if you don't look at the individual as the problem. Instead, look at *his or her* problems. What does this individual need to make the workday more successful and worklife more joyful? Here are eleven truisms related to performance; some of them are centuries old, but they are as true today as ever.

Truism 1: No one takes a job to fail

Your employees took on their present responsibilities with high hopes of fulfilling them successfully. If one of those employees is not succeeding, she or he is lacking one of these performance basics:

- Clarity regarding performance expectations
- A clear picture of what excellent performance looks like
- An understanding that there is a gap between her or his performance and the performance expectations
- Tools or needs such as knowledge, skill, motivation, workspace enhancement, or tactical coaching.

In each of these four situations, you as a manager or supervisor can help.

- You can clarify performance expectations by setting clear, measurable goals and objectives, as described in Chapter 2.
- You can offer coaching, job shadowing, or demonstrations to show the employee exactly what great performance looks like.
- You can candidly, descriptively, and humanely point out the gaps between the employee's performance and the performance expectations. Too many employees have lost their jobs because managers do not have the courage to address performance shortfalls until it is too late.
- In almost every case, you can aid the employee in fulfilling his or her needs. If the employee lacks knowledge or skills, you can offer coaching or training. If the workspace or tools are a deterrent to top performance, often a manager can make some modifications or purchases. If motivation is lacking, then it is within the manager's power to administer rewards or consequences.

The employee probably wants to improve his or her performance even more than the manager does, but outward appearances may be deceiving. Make no mistake: Every employee would rather succeed than fail. Outwardly, the employee may project an "I don't care" attitude in order to mask feelings of insecurity. Leaders who are not daunted by first impressions of performance problems can set organizations on the path to great performance. Managers have more power than they think they have.

This book identifies dozens of performance problems and offers a variety of solutions to each. Then, hundreds of creative and realistic techniques are given in detail to help managers turn around common workplace problems. By using these interventions to solve an employee's performance problem, the manager immediately improves the work life of the employee, as well as that of the team. High-performing individuals build high-performing teams and increase productivity and profits.

Truism 2: People are motivated by two things: fear of punishment and hope of reward

Although this book offers some motivational solutions that are based on consequences, most of the solutions are rewarding to the employee in some way. Few of these rewards or incentives involve money. Today's employees, especially, are motivated by so many things: flexible work hours, training to enhance their worth in the marketplace, a family-friendly work environment, the desire to make a contribution to society, and much, much more. These interventions capitalize on every employee's desire to find rewarding work and to be appreciated and acknowledged.

Truism 3: Small performance problems that are not addressed early become big problems and can spread to good performers

Most employees don't work in a silo. They unconsciously benchmark their performance against the performance of others. If poor performers are not turned around, the standards of the other employees around them slowly deteriorate.

Truism 4: If you do what you always do, you will get what you've always gotten

Managers who do not try new approaches to changing behaviors and boosting performance do not lead people forward. Not only does the company not benefit from greater productivity, but the employees do not increase their skills or their professionalism. Many recruiters are noting that today's sought-after employees are citing professional development as one of the benefits they are looking for in their next job. Savvy employees want a company that will support them in increasing their skills and competencies.

Expectations are high these days. No one is satisfied with duplicating the performance of the past. Companies are seeking avenues to even greater productivity. Abraham Maslow, the founder of the science of behavior, once said, "To the man who has only a hammer, everything begins to look like a nail." Likewise, if a manager has been trying to achieve performance results with the same five methods for years, that manager will think that those five methods hold the answers to all performance problems. Methods of performance improvement include the following:

- Training
- Goal setting and evaluation
- Performance appraisal and review
- Performance management and measurement
- Professional development strategies

- 360° instruments and feedback
- Incentives and rewards
- Meaningful consequences/positive discipline
- Problem solving
- Coaching and counseling

This list is just the beginning of the many opportunities managers have to make all kinds of employees successful. You are urged to experiment, to try new approaches, and to work to challenge employees in surprising new ways by using the numerous interventions in this book.

Truism 5: Everybody is good at something—the trick is to find out what each person is good at

One of the approaches to changing performance used in this book is to change the environment, the tools, the assignment, or some other external factor instead of changing the employee. Most solutions to performance problems depend on changing the performer, but some of the book's interventions encourage managers to realign *tasks* with the *gifts* of the performer. Although this is not always possible, particularly in small organizations, redistributing assignments to make everyone more successful is a tactic that managers should at least consider. Reassigning should be undertaken with this caveat, however: Make no changes that somehow penalize good performers or burden them with undesirable duties cast off by poor performers. Use these interventions when the realignment works for all the employees affected.

In some cases, managers may find two employees who enjoy very different things about their jobs. For example, a customer service position may entail 50 percent customer contact and 50 percent administrative tasks. If an employee is not performing well with customers, the two jobs could be redesigned so that one job would be totally customer contact and the other would handle all administrative duties. Redesigning the roles of both employees this way, however, works only if the good performer wants to have 100 percent customer contact. If the good performer loves that role, the redesign is a great intervention and offers promise that the poor performer will be more successful in the administrative role. If, however, the good performer likes the balance between customer contact and administrative work, he should not be penalized by having his job altered to "reward" a poor performer. Keep this in mind as you review interventions that alter the jobs of other employees or that require peer coaching.

Truism 6: You can't please a boss who doesn't know what she wants

Pogo made famous the statement, "We have met the enemy and he is us." Some managers are their own worst enemies when it comes to endeavoring to improve performance. The manager may want performance to be better in general, but does not have specific goals or performance descriptions in mind. Or, she may make the mistake of thinking that the employee sees performance and standards exactly as she does. The two may actually have extremely different views of acceptable performance based on different past experiences.

Asking an employee to meet a performance expectation without a vivid description of what "good" looks like is akin to asking an archer to hit a bulls-eye without allowing the archer to see the target. First, managers need to get a concrete image of what good performance looks like and then draw the employee a picture. For some employees, drawing a vivid picture of good performance is the only intervention needed.

Every person's view of his or her performance has been shaped by former employers and managers, parents, challenging or unchallenging school systems, peer groups, and dozens of other factors. A manager is responsible for depicting the target performance in action words and descriptors that the employee can readily grasp.

Truism 7: Sometimes the best course of action is no action at all

In many chapters, managers are urged to pause and consider the very valuable option of doing nothing at all. Some unproductive employee behaviors are temporary and result from a specific circumstance at work or at home. If the employee has proven valuable in other ways in the past, leaving him to work out the behavior on his own may be the most efficient route to returning the employee to top performance. At the same time, the manager should communicate to the employee that she is expecting the behavior to change. Otherwise, the small performance problem may become larger or permanent.

Truism 8: Catch people doing something right

In *The One Minute Manager*, Ken Blanchard made famous the supervision technique of "catching people doing something right." He showed how easy it is for human nature to prompt us to point out the flaws and imperfections of performance and how much more challenging it is to pinpoint things that an employee is doing well. The powerful force of positive reinforcement is unleashed in many of the interventions in this book. In recent years, management has come to realize that focusing repetitively on what an employee is doing wrong plants a picture of bad performance in an employee's mind. It is more effective to capture really great performances, recognize them, and point them out. This reinforces great performance for the employees and their peers instead of solely calling attention to poor performance. Employees focus on the details of a great performance and what it feels like. *201 Ways to Turn Any Employee into a Star Performer* shares a variety of ways to use this turbo-booster for performance.

Truism 9: You get greater performance shoulder to shoulder than standing over someone

John D. Rockefeller once said:

> I have long been convinced that in the very nature of things, employers and employees are partners, not enemies; that their interests are common, not opposed; that in the long run the success of one depends on the success of the other.

Although active, strong leadership is encouraged throughout this book, an attitude of partnering is prevalent; there is as much asking as telling, and the communication is always two-way. Other methods may get the job done today, but partnering is the only way to achieve top performance over the long term. Developing and retaining great performers is the mission of every chapter of this book.

Employees have to take the lead in turning around their performance, from diagnosing the problems to creating realistic but challenging goals for improvement.

Truism 10: It takes different strokes for different folks

One of the most valuable revolutions of the past decade in education is adapting to various learning styles for more effective results. Business needs to take notice. The key to teaching employees new skills is determining whether a worker learns best by reading directions, watching a demonstration, or putting her hands to a task and learning by trial and error. Simply observing or remembering times when the employee seemed to learn quickly and enjoy the process can give clues about the employee's learning style. Asking an employee how he wishes to be trained or coached sometimes works. Some training, like product knowledge, can be put on CDs for auditory learners. The same information can be put in manuals or on slides, DVDs, or videos for visual learners. Using the way the employee takes in information best can save both the employee and the employer from the frustration of having to repeat lessons and specifications; such repetition causes both teacher and student to feel like failures.

Truism 11: You can't just talk the talk; you must walk the walk

Today's employees expect authenticity in their leaders. If you require a high standard, whether in ethics, production, or quality, then you must demonstrate your commitment to that standard as well. Now more than ever, employees want models of performance. Take care that you model the behaviors and demonstrate a commitment to the goals that you expect from others.

EVERYTHING YOU NEED TO TURN AROUND PROBLEM PERFORMERS

The following chapters offer strategies, tools, and, in some cases, even scripts for turning around problem performance. The first four chapters of the book offer understanding of performance and approaches for making positive and lasting changes. Everything from creating winning goals that boost productivity to creating a long-term plan for an employee's ongoing development are offered in a succinct and easy-to-implement style.

Each of Chapters 5 through 19 deals with a specific performance problem. You can choose from a generous array of interventions for working with great employees, not-so-great employees, and the worst employees. The diversity in choices allows managers to find the approach that they feel most comfortable implementing and that they think best fits their unique employee and workplace. In its entirety, *201 Ways to Turn Any Employee into a Star Performer* equips managers to transform behaviors so that every employee can achieve a productive work life.

The interventions have been designed for today's employees and today's workplace, because both have changed radically in recent years. Whether managers are looking for new approaches to old problems or a quick education on dealing with very recent problems such as Internet abuse, the following chapters offer techniques that are easy to grasp and implement. Interventions are explicit, and the information is easy to access. Using the recommended interventions will put both the employee and the employer on a road to stellar performance, and that success will enhance both profits and personal satisfaction.

2

Creating Goals for Turnaround

A great goal offers an employee the opportunity to succeed, but the word *goal* also implies a stretch to achieve that success. Managers generally err on one side of this definition or the other. Some make the goal too lofty. When the employee realizes that he can never achieve the goal, he ceases to take it seriously. Other managers do not set true goals. What they call goals are actually just descriptions of the employee's current responsibilities. Such goals foster more of the same performance, the status quo. Without challenging goals, the individual misses an opportunity to grow professionally, resulting in lost productivity for the company.

THE SMART MODEL

The standard for goals in most organizations is the SMART model.

S   Specific

M   Measurable

A   Action-oriented and Aggressive

R   Realistic

T   Timed

Each of these elements is necessary if a goal is to be meaningful. Goals are worthless if there is no way to follow through and use them as benchmarks for performance. The elements of the SMART goal model give the manager and the employee an infrastructure for building improved performance in the following ways.

Specific goals

Specific goals are necessary so that employees understand exactly what is expected of them. Amazingly, some employees are clueless about standards of quality or productivity. Experienced managers have learned, usually the hard way, that some employees do not perform well because no one has ever shown them exactly what a good performance looks like. The following examples show the difference between a specific goal and a nonspecific goal.

Nonspecific goal:

Process a satisfactory number of forms per day.

Specific goal:

Process a minimum of 85 expense forms per day, with fewer than 4 being returned to reprocess, and include typed comments.

The specific numbers, the quality standards, and the expectation of comments in the second example spell out what the manager expects. The employee will know exactly what is expected of her and will have a benchmark for her performance.

Measurable goals

Designing *measurable goals* is challenging for some professions. What if the employee is in a sales organization that closes only one or two major sales per year? The employee still needs incremental goals. A measurable goal for such a sales professional could be to make five phone calls daily to potential new customers, make three follow-up calls to existing customers, and send five emails introducing new products. Weekly, the sales professional could be required to send one proposal and five sales letters. Having measurable goals allows the employee to be evaluated on his performance in more ways than just revenue brought in. A manager who uses measurable goals can more quickly identify employees who are having problems that are interfering with performance. In the case of this sales professional, the manager would not need to wait until the end of the year to discern that the employee was not going to make any money for himself or for the company. By comparing performance to measurable goals, the manager could see much earlier that the employee was heading for trouble. *201 Ways to Turn Any Employee into a Star Performer* offers interventions that can be implemented as soon as the manager realizes that performance is not measuring up to goals.

Action-oriented and aggressive goals

Action-oriented goals that are *aggressive* are the goals that ignite great performance. Performance does not improve when a manager uses descriptive terms like *high-quality, energetic,* or *proactive.* Performance improves when a manager tells an employee what she must do in order to achieve her goals. Note that the goals given in the previous examples use action verbs, telling employees what they must "process," "type," "email," or "call."

The aggressive part of the SMART model gives the employee something to strive for. It should represent a higher standard of performance than the employee is currently achieving. If an employee does not have the bar set a bit higher each time, that employee never develops her or his own value in the marketplace. Also, employees who don't improve their performance over time build companies that get left behind in the increasingly competitive marketplace. Aggressive goals are today called *stretch goals* in most organizations. The idea is akin to weight training: By adding a little more weight or repetition, an individual can build himself up and be stronger and more effective. Similarly, putting an individual under a little pressure to push harder and achieve more builds up her ability to achieve greater things.

Realistic goals

Being *realistic* is just as important as being *aggressive* in creating goals that make people better at their jobs. To continue the weight-training analogy, adding a realistic amount of weight and gradually increasing the demands on a body builds up muscle and endurance. If the demands are ramped up too much too fast, however, the body can actually be damaged. The same is true with realistic and unrealistic goals. Adding excessive pressure to encourage an employee to improve performance too much too fast can actually damage performance. An employee may experience a feeling of failure, and performance will surely suffer. Instead of giving the employee an incentive through a stretch goal, you will have given the employee a disincentive through a ridiculous expectation. Even great employees who actually succeed in achieving aggressive goals that are too challenging will probably burn out or find another job with a more realistic pace.

Before you create a goal, assess where your employee is in terms of performance and then add a little more pressure to perform. Avoid dangerously overburdening the employee. Ask the employee to do a little more or build in some specific quality expectations that raise the standard. Don't throw everything at the employee at once. Employees improve best when they focus on improving in one area at a time.

Timed goals

Timed goals set an expectation for the employee and the manager that the goal is to be completed or perfected by a certain time. Some employees can achieve quality standards if they are given a year, but the organization may need that type of performance in a month. For example, an employee may be given the goal of creating a strategic plan for marketing. If he is given no time limit, he may take a year to gather the information and create the plan. By that time, so many changes may have occurred that the plan will not be as useful. If the employee is given 90 days to create the plan, that steps up the level of performance expectations quite a bit.

Some goals may even have hourly time constraints. A call center employee for a financial services firm may be expected to take 12 calls per hour. Building in an hourly expectation makes clear to the employee that she is expected to use her time to accomplish a dozen calls and not the number of calls that makes her comfortable. The goal also gives the employee a target, and employees historically perform at a much higher level when they are aiming at a target.

THE GOAL-SETTING PROCESS

How you set goals has as much to do with their successful achievement as how you write them. Each manager will develop a style that works best for him or her, but one process that works particularly well is given here.

Step one

First, the manager acquaints the employee with the departmental goals set down by management or by the company's business plan. The manager may share the vision or objectives as well so that the employee realizes that her or his performance is important to the success of the entire organization. This introduction to the bigger picture may take place in a staff meeting or one-on-one.

Step two

The second step must be conducted one-on-one with the employee. The employee is given a sheet of paper with a large circle on it. The manager asks the employee to divide the circle into wedges like a pie. The entire pie equals a 40-hour workweek. Each wedge represents a block of time during the week that is used to perform a particular task or responsibility. A very small wedge might represent the 1 hour a week that the employee spends on completing expense reports. A larger wedge might represent the 6 hours a week spent in internal meetings. A wedge twice that size represents the 12 hours a week spent on phone calls with customers. Be sure the employee does this exercise in pencil, as he or she will probably make lots of changes. Encourage the employee to just make a best guess and not to worry about an exact representation of his or her week.

After the pie has been completely divided up, set it aside. Tell the employee that you will be getting back to it at a later time, but for now you want to switch tracks.

Step three

Bring out the departmental goals and objectives, and ask the employee to review them with you again. Ask the employee if she or he sees any of these goals and objectives as being particularly challenging for the team. After much discussion, ask the employee to take the departmental goals and create her or his own goals for the next year, using the SMART model. Ask the employee what portion of each departmental goal he or she is willing to take responsibility for. For example, if your department of three sales representatives is charged with adding at least 10 new accounts a month, a good response from the employee would be that he will be responsible for adding 4 of those accounts. On the other hand, if your goal is to increase revenue by 20 percent, every employee will need to commit to increasing the revenue he or she brings in by 20 percent or more. If the goal is to have only 3 out of 50 data input sheets returned because of errors, a manager would hope that an experienced employee would set a personal goal of only 2 out of 50, since new hires are likely to have more errors than average.

After the first goal is complete, create an individual goal for each of the remaining departmental goals. Add any personal or professional development goals that you think are appropriate.

Step four

Now review the pie representing how the employee's time is used. Ask the employee what wedges he or she needs to increase or spend more time on in order to meet stretch goals. Ask whether he or she can trim the amount of time spent on activities that are not as productive. Brainstorm ways to help the employee be more productive. If costs are not prohibitive, offer to buy tools or training that will support the employee's efforts. Redistribute the time on the pie chart.

Step five

With the employee, review the goals that she or he has written using the SMART model. Encourage the employee to stretch more in some areas if you see opportunities for growth. Make sure every goal is Specific, Measurable, Action-oriented and Aggressive, Realistic, and Timed. If any one of these elements is left out, collaborate with the employee to write it in.

Step six

Set a time to get back together with the employee to compare the employee's actual performance with the goals set. Take each goal and decide whether every action was taken successfully and within the time constraints. If a goal has not been met, ask the employee to identify barriers to successful completion of that goal. Occasionally, things like natural disasters or mergers make adhering to the original plan impossible. In most cases, however, goals should be achieved or exceeded. If they are not, it is time to use the information in the following chapters to upgrade performance.

GOALS ARE NOT AN ANNUAL EVENT

Goals should not be looked upon as an event, but rather as an ongoing process. After goals have been collaboratively set and mutually agreed upon, they should be referred to and discussed routinely as part of the workday. Great performance is usually achieved when the goals are uppermost on the performer's mind every day. It is the manager's responsibility to ensure that no employee ever gets close to annual review time and remembers his or her goals for the first time since last year. Those goals should be the basis of encouragement, accountability, and many conversations throughout each quarter.

The performance review, a more formal conversation, is addressed more fully in the next chapter.

3

Stellar Long-Term Performance: The Performance Appraisal and Development Plan

You would worry about an employee with average ability who started with your company as a mail delivery clerk, performed well, and 30 years later retired from the same position. That is an extreme example of an employee who was never developed. Some development occurs naturally as employees learn on the job and prepare to be promoted to higher positions. But most development has nothing to do with promotions or raises. Most development is in the area of professional growth. Today companies have trimmed layers of management, so opportunities for advancement up a career ladder are few and usually years apart. New-millennium employees have learned to look for movement in their careers through developmental moves. They value learning new technical or tactical skills, they make more lateral moves or job rotations to broaden their experience, and they have higher expectations that an employer will train them and invest in them.

Two tools for improving people's skills are the performance appraisal and the development plan. Both will improve an employee's abilities to meet goals and improve organizational performance. More important, employees will feel gratified, valued, and more loyal when these two processes are conducted. If you want to develop high-performing employees, conducting life-changing performance appraisals is a must. Second only to the performance appraisal is the development plan that every employee should have. Motivation and goal setting take care of getting tasks done today or this quarter. Performance appraisals and development plans build stellar performance that lasts and improves each year. The benefits of these two initiatives are of enduring value and well worth the extra time that a manager invests; payback from these efforts is realized year after year.

THE PERFORMANCE APPRAISAL

The performance appraisal takes the goals created with the employee and evaluates how the employee is performing relative to those goals. Just like the goal-setting session, the performance appraisal is a joint effort between the employer and the employee. Start with the assumption that the employee wants to perform well. If the employee has not met her or his goals, work with her or him as a partner to solve the problem. Evaluate the reasons why the employee is not as successful as he or she would wish to be (and as you would wish him or her to be). Performance appraisals, handled correctly, can come to be regarded by employees as an investment in their professional development and careers.

Unfortunately, many managers are not skilled in conducting performance appraisals, so many employees regard these sessions as threatening. Surveys show that managers dread conducting a performance appraisal even more than they dread having their own performance appraised. (This should make employees feel more relaxed, knowing the boss is more nervous than they are!) Managers may feel uncomfortable delivering information about goals that have not been met. They may fear confrontation or an unpredictable employee response. And many managers know that they have not prepared consistently throughout the quarter or the year to deliver a meaningful and constructive performance appraisal. That's a lot of negativity for a manager to carry into any employee meeting; little wonder these meetings can get emotional at times.

Performance appraisals can go particularly awry if the company ties the appraisal to compensation, a supercharged topic. If at all possible, try to hold conversations about compensation at a separate time from the performance appraisal. The appraisal should be valued as something that is done *for* the employee, not *to* the employee. Your company will have its unique way of dealing with compensation, but try to divorce those conversations from the time set aside for planning for improved performance.

Consider this: When a young employee accepts his first position, does he do so with the desire to be exactly as skilled and proficient in 10 years as he is on Day One? Of course not. It is his hope that managers along the way will teach him new skills, improve the skill set he starts with, and offer him some new challenges. Yet some managers are hesitant to challenge employees and set expectations nudging them to increase their proficiency and skill. This may be because some managers have a greater need to be liked by employees than to lead them. Ironically, however, most people seem to like those bosses who demanded their best— within reason.

THE STEP-BY-STEP PROCESS

The performance appraisal process discussed here offers opportunities for both the manager and the employee to contribute to the employee's enhanced performance. Each manager will modify this process and make it fit his or her personality and company. Be sure that you include any steps specific to your industry and to meet all requirements set down by your human resources department.

Preparing for the meeting

The manager should pull together all performance-related information. This information should be as objective as possible, usually based on results in the workplace. The manager should compare the performance results with the employee's goals and develop some performance objectives from that. Especially note any area where the employee is *exceeding* goals. The performance appraisal is not intended to be punitive, but rather to offer the employee constructive feedback about her or his total performance—particularly good performance. Some managers fear that complimenting employees on a positive performance will make them decrease their effort. In most cases, the opposite is true. If tasks that are done well are not acknowledged and only the negative performance is discussed, experienced managers note that the good performance often deteriorates from neglect. In addition, a total focus on the negative will leave employees demoralized, and they may start looking for a job elsewhere.

The following are examples of performance results that might be compared against goals:

- Number of documents processed
- Revenue brought in or managed
- Number of phone calls or emails related to a particular task
- Number of sales or contracts
- Reduction/increase in mistakes
- New ideas or new projects initiated
- Accuracy of projections or forecasts
- Deadlines met or missed
- Consistency in coverage of responsibility
- Quality checks—improved or not
- Customer complaints/compliments/requests
- Doing more work with fewer people or resources
- Amount of new business/number of seized opportunities
- Activity: meetings or training attended/appointments/events
- Skill certification or measurable change
- Proposals or reports written
- Problems solved
- New products or services
- Improved performance of other employees
- Number of tasks performed

Since measures were put in place through the SMART goals from Chapter 2, the manager has the tools to tell the employee how he or she is doing, something that every employee has the right to know but sometimes doesn't.

Opening the meeting

Open the meeting by telling the employee three things and asking him or her a very important question:

- Why you value the employee—in specific ways.
- Your commitment to the employee's career and his or her development, not just in this meeting, but for the long term. (The only time you might not want to say these things is if you believe the employee will be terminated at some time in the future.)
- In this busy work environment, how much you welcome the opportunity to sit and focus on the employee's career, performance, and needs.
- Then ask the employee how he or she feels about this meeting or if he or she has any other expectations. Address whatever the employee says; be sure to be responsive.

The employee self-appraises first

Give the employee a copy of her or his goals and ask the employee to give an assessment of how she or he is doing. Do not interrupt; allow the employee to say everything that is on his or her mind, even if you disagree. In many cases, employees are more critical of their performance than their manager is. If the employee asks if you agree and you don't, say that you will address all items when the employee has finished.

Discuss areas of agreement first

Take one goal on which you both agree that the employee is doing well. Give feedback about how well the employee has done. Use specific measures to back up why you have evaluated the employee highly in this area. Add to that any areas where you might have evaluated the employee higher than he or she rated him- or herself. If you have difficulty getting employees to evaluate themselves, try having them evaluate their performance of every goal on a scale of 1 to 10, with 10 being "greatly exceeds all expectations" and 1 being "poor performance."

Discuss areas where the employee needs more improvement than she or he realizes

Be very objective—never subjective. Start by saying, "I would like for us to discuss some of the goals that have not been met, and I see that your estimation is a bit higher than mine." It is acceptable to say that the departmental norm (and the employee's goal) is to evaluate 10 MRIs per day and that the employee is averaging only 8, indicating a need to improve productivity. It is not acceptable to say that the employee doesn't seem to work at a steady pace unless you have concrete information to back that up. Your comments may be no surprise and may even be appreciated. On the other hand, you may provoke hostility, irritability, or even tears. This does not mean that you have failed. Some people walk in with so much tension from outside the job that the least bit of discouraging feedback sets them off. On the other hand, if you are getting predominantly negative responses, you should consider taking a class in conducting performance reviews, such as the one taught by the author of this book.

Whatever the response, use plenty of empathy statements as you work through all the areas that need improvement. An empathy statement follows this formula:

You must feel _____ because _____.

The first blank should be filled with a word that guesses at what the employee must be feeling: frustrated, relieved, proud, disappointed, concerned, surprised, regretful, or some other emotional description. The second part of the sentence is filled with something from the performance appraisal that has evoked the emotion. The word *because* may be replaced with *since* or *that*. Some sample empathy statements follow:

- You must feel *disappointed* because there is a gap between your evaluation and mine.
- You must feel *let down* that you were not able to meet your goal of zero rework this quarter.
- You must feel *at the top of your game,* since you were able to meet every goal.

Be open to amending your evaluation of the employee. For example, a manager may forget that she relieved an employee of some responsibility so that the employee could help with an unexpected task that arose. In that case, it may not be the employee's fault that the original goal was not met. Hard feelings and poor performance may follow if the manager does not verbalize her change in appraisal to recognize a valid point that the employee makes. Saying "I'm wrong" will increase the employee's respect for the manager, not decrease it.

Performance appraisals may include numerical evaluations that rate the employee's performance. Your company will decide which style is best for you and should provide instruction in how to implement whatever performance tools or forms it has adopted.

Focus on the future: developing an action plan

The last part of the meeting should be an optimistic look at the employee's future performance. If the employee has not met some goals, establish what the employee needs: training, coaching from you, new tools or environmental changes, better time management, fewer distractions, or help in the form of one of the interventions given in later chapters of this book. Say, "The rest of this meeting will be focused on both of us making some commitments to making you successful at reaching your goals. This is what I understand that you need from me and what I can offer to do." (Cite any help that you are able and willing to give.) "What commitments are you prepared to make in order to reach these goals?" (Ensure that the employee takes all the responsibilities he or she should.) "Those commitments should be very constructive in reaching your goals. In addition, I am asking that you _____." (Cite other commitments that you expect from the employee.)

Document everything from this meeting

In addition, some managers end by creating one of the following:

- A new set of goals. Goals may be increased or amended based on the employee's needs.
- A contract documenting what both the employee and you have agreed to do in order to increase performance.

- A development plan to ensure continued professional growth for the employee and enhanced long-term performance.

Whatever you do, document all the key points that you made to the employee, along with the employee's responses and commitments. Documentation is useful to hold yourself accountable and as a reminder as you manage the employee to achieve greater performance. Documentation is also necessary if disciplinary action is needed later.

Thank the employee

Thank the employee for the serious effort that she or he put into the performance appraisal and end by stating your confidence in the employee's ability to achieve even greater things in the future. Add one compliment that is very specific about the employee's performance.

This is not the only process for conducting a performance appraisal, but it is one of the most positive ones. Keep in mind that a manager can never improve an employee's performance; only the employee can do that. Employees walk out of this performance appraisal with all the information they need to improve their performance. More important, they walk out empowered, supported, and forward-looking instead of feeling like failures.

THE DEVELOPMENT PLAN

Performance appraisals focus on short-term performance. The development plan focuses on developing the employee's skills, traits, abilities, and experience for the following long-term purposes:

- Increase the employee's value to the company
- Increase the employee's professionalism and competencies
- Increase the employee's marketplace value and ability to take on greater responsibility within the company

Manangers' reasons for not spending resources on long-term development are many, and are usually based on the following myths.

Myth	Truth about Development
People will leave once they acquire new skills.	• Good people will leave anyway, in all probability. They will get a promotion or a chance at more responsibility. If you train and develop employees, they are more likely to stay within your company. It's better to lose a great employee to another position in your own company than to another company. • Grooming people from within for that next position allows you to hire talented people from within—and their learning curve is shorter!
There is no payback from long-term development.	• On the contrary, you will bring money to the bottom line with development. Top performers list working for a company that develops its people ahead of many perks—including company cars! This results in savings in recruiting, orientation, and training. Turnover costs money, and development reduces turnover. • Skills and experiences developed will probably be needed in a future job; nothing is ever wasted. • You increase the value of existing employees when you develop them.
Development takes the employee off the job and hurts productivity.	• Job satisfaction and productivity are increased in organizations that develop their people. • Mistakes and rework decrease when employees are developed. • No employee works every minute of a workday; less time is spent on negative talk and furtive job searches when employees have something more worthwhile to do—like developmental steps.
Development takes too much of a manager's valuable time.	• Managers will either spend the time in development or spend the time fixing problems that result from not developing people. It's better to spend time doing positive management tasks. • Communication, team building, and many other managerial tasks are accomplished simultaneously when development takes place.

PREPARING TO WRITE A DEVELOPMENT PLAN

Before creating the development plan, it is advisable to gather as much information about the employee as possible. Some excellent sources of information that can be accessed for the development plan are as follows:

- Performance appraisals or reviews
- Goals and objectives
- 360° feedback (peers, subordinates, boss)
- Any skill evaluations
- Statistics like revenue or production numbers
- Other productivity or performance information

CREATING THE PLAN

Begin by writing down all the needs the employee has

What does the employee need in order to be more successful and to prepare for that next step up in your organization? List those developmental needs.

List the intervention or developmental step you will take to meet each of the employee's needs

Training, coaching by managers or peers, field trips to other companies, and other methods offer employees means of development. List one or, preferably, more steps that you will take to ensure that the employee's performance becomes more proficient in one area. If you can make time, it is helpful to give the employee information regarding where he or she can go to get the developmental resources. For example, if a book on tape is brought up in the performance review, list the number of your corporate library or the URL of a media provider.

Craft a development plan that lists the steps to take for career and professional development for at least a year

Include resources, dates, and other helpful information. A sample development plan follows.

DEVELOPMENTAL PLAN
2003

John Doe
Engineering Services
Benjamin Jones, Senior Vice President

Developmental Step	Resources	Developmental Needs
Self-Directed Learning		
1. A. Subscribe to and read one of the following magazines regularly. • *Engineering Management Quarterly* • *Public Utility Fortnightly* B. Summarize one article that you found interesting and route it to your peers and selected subordinates. Do this quarterly.	1. Large local bookstore such as Oxford Books or Borders, 704-7900	1. Broaden your professional scope. View the business more globally. Apply trends and future directions to your area and your career.
2. Read *Techno Trends* by Daniel Burruss. Discuss it with a peer or manager.	2. JEL Resources, 746-0764	2. Begin to think more strategically about our work process. How can technology change the way we manage, now and in the future?
3. View one or more of the following videos and discuss it with a peer: • Less Stress in Four Easy Steps • Mentoring Works	3. NPC Library, 426-6847	3. Development in this area is ongoing. • As rate of change and stress factors increase, learn a variety of ways to handle stress on the job.

Developmental Step	Resources	Developmental Needs
		• Continue to mentor others in the organization in order to develop them and yourself.

Experiential Learning

4. Set up a half-day tour of some area of marketing that interests you. For, example: Accompany a marketing segment manager on a customer call or work with a Marketing Communications staffer on a trade show.	4. Marketing professional of your choice.	4. Broaden your scope. Learn more about other areas of the company and how we integrate.
5. Check out a self-paced computer course from I.S.	5. Information Services, 406-4090	5. Continue to prepare for future roles in the company by enhancing your computer skills.

Coaching: Peers/Subordinates/Consultants

6. Set up two or three meetings or lunches over the next quarter with Ellen Hay. Ask her to serve as your peer coach on integrated services. Prepare specific questions to ask her.	6. Ellen Hay, Transmission Services	6. Increase your knowledge of ITS.
7. Set up similar meetings with Don Ford.	7. Don Ford	7. Increase your expertise in evaluating and reading contracts.

(Continues)

(*Continued*)

DEVELOPMENTAL PLAN

Developmental Step	Resources	Developmental Needs
Development by Manager		
8. Accompany your manager to a meeting or event that will offer you increased exposure. Ask your manager to select a good opportunity this quarter.	8. Ron Hawley	8. Increase your exposure to other areas of the company. Increase your versatility.
Training		
9. Attend seminar, Washington, D.C.	9. Online Resources	9. Explore how entities outside the United States influence our business. Begin to view the business more globally.
10. Attend Student of the Business course.	10. Synesis University, 426-5644	10. Broaden your scope of the industry and your role in it.

FOLLOW-UP IS THE KEY TO RESULTS

Putting a plan into the employee's hands is only the first step. Now the real work begins for both the employee and the manager. Implementation, reinforcement, and encouragement are the critical parts of development. Check in with the employee periodically to ensure that he or she is continuing to develop as planned. Ask the employee about various developmental steps from the plan and how she or he is fulfilling them.

With the development plan as a long-term tool for lasting performance and the performance appraisal to manage present performance, the manager may avoid many of the performance problems described in the later chapters of this book. Heading off problems by developing star performers from the outset is by far the best strategy for creating stellar teams and high-performing companies.

4

Stopping Problems at the First Sign: Motivation to Change

Every employee has certain inalienable rights regarding the management of his or her performance. Whether these rights are ever mentioned or not, every employee feels innately entitled to these basic expectations. And any manager who violates these rights finds out very quickly how strongly employees feel that these are not rights to be taken lightly. Most of these rights relate to feedback about performance, which is the cornerstone of motivation. To ensure motivation, take great care to deliver timely communication regarding how well each employee is performing in relation to her or his goals. If you do not, you will have violated one of the rights discussed in this chapter.

EMPLOYEE RIGHTS TO PERFORMANCE FEEDBACK

The right to know when performance falls short of or exceeds expectations

Tell the employee when there is a gap between acceptable performance and current performance. Employees are fired every day who could have been salvaged and made into valuable contributors if someone had communicated to them that they needed to change. The workplace loses too many skilled employees this way. Just as critical to a successful workforce is letting great performers know that their performance is spectacular. Everyone needs some type of reinforcement. If you think that not mentioning an employee's extraordinary performance will keep that employee humble and motivated, you are very wrong. Some employees exceed expectations just to garner that feedback. If they do not receive it, they stop giving as much.

The right to receive feedback as soon as possible when performance does not measure up to management's expectations

There is nothing to be gained by delaying feedback on poor performance, but consider all that can be lost. First, the time that will be lost as the poor performance continues will cost your company money and perhaps have a negative impact on quality. Second, the poorly performing employee is not the only person affected, since most people don't work in a vacuum. Other employees may be hampered by this employee's inefficiencies, or their own performance may deteriorate. Customer service may suffer, and internal partners or allies may experience problems. Third, telling the employee as soon as possible may keep a very small problem from developing into a bad habit. Conversely, nothing has the emotional zing of praising a job well done at the moment it is completed.

No employee should be passed on, passed over, or fired until he or she has received performance feedback and has been given the chance to improve

In many organizations, employees are not given timely feedback on poor performance because their managers are uncomfortable about saying anything negative. Instead, the managers pass poorly performing employees on to other departments. The company still loses productivity every day, since the employee's performance has not improved.

An even greater disservice has been done to these employees. They have not been given the chance to succeed because they are unaware that they have a performance gap. Other employees who don't get dumped on other departments stay in the same position and wonder why they are not being cultivated for greater roles. Employees should be told what elements of their behavior need improving so that they can remedy that behavior and remove the barriers to their success.

A still greater disservice is done to those employees who are terminated without having been given the opportunity to work through their problems. Some managers seethe over poor performance but don't communicate their dismay to the employee. These managers often think the employee just somehow knows that there is a problem. Suddenly, one day, the manager finds an excuse to terminate such an employee and grabs that opportunity. The manager would rather fire the employee than specifically describe the areas where the employee's performance falls short. This sounds strange, but exit interviews reveal that it happens all too frequently.

The right to work toward remedying poor performance

Once the performance feedback has been delivered to the employee, she or he should have a reasonable amount of time to correct the performance. During this period, the employee should receive coaching, counseling, support, and tools from management to aid in successful rehabilitation.

The right to receive performance feedback in private and with open two-way communication

Employees who have too much pride or have no self-worth at all will usually suffer if they receive criticism in front of a peer. Even the most balanced employees will hear, retain, and respond to feedback better if it is delivered privately. More important, the employee should feel that she or he is encouraged to respond, ask questions, and receive answers following the feedback. Simply telling an employee that he or she is doing something wrong is rarely effective. The two-way communication and positive reinforcement that follows performance feedback are as critical as the feedback itself.

TIMELY PERFORMANCE FEEDBACK

Chapters 5 through 19 contain hundreds of interventions designed to improve performance. Managers must use great wisdom in choosing the correct intervention for each individual employee and organization.

Looking at the full scope of any performance problem helps determine where the problem starts:

- Is it a coaching problem (i.e., can the manager or a peer coach the employee through it)?
- Is it a counseling problem (i.e., should the manager communicate with the employee and issue an incentive or consequence)?
- Is it an opportunity for a problem-solving session?
- Is it an environmental problem that a change in the office, the tools, or the process will remedy for the employee?
- Does the problem lie more with the manager than with the employee, and does the employee have permission to communicate freely upward?

Managers should consider all of these factors before implementing an intervention.

PINPOINTING PERFORMANCE PROBLEMS

The first step in solving a performance problem is to conduct a problem analysis. A problem analysis holds a problem up to the light, looks at it from every angle, and asks the following questions:

- What is the performance problem? Examples: tardiness, absenteeism, conflict.
- What are the barriers to good performance? Examples: early work hours, sick children to care for, poor communication skills. This step helps managers see if the problem is entirely employee performance or if it may be environmental or management-related. The manager then brainstorms ways to remove any barriers. Interventions in this book offer creative ways to remove barriers to top performance.
- What are the drivers for good performance? Examples: desire for approval, fear of losing job, frustration from poor relationships on the job. The manager reviews all the forces driving positive change and finds ways to reinforce those positive forces and use them for rewards.

ASSESSING THE NEEDS OF PERFORMERS

No discussion of performance would be complete without an understanding of Mager's work on assessing performance problems. Robert Mager, through his Center for Effective Performance, has done some of the most valuable work in performance management of the last two decades. Put into simplest terms, Mager begins with two questions:

1. Can the performer do the task or can he not? (Does the performer have the skills, abilities, strength, and raw resources?)
2. Will the performer do the task or won't he? (If the employee has the ability to complete the task, does she or he have an attitudinal or volitional reluctance to perform?)

A matrix can be drawn from these two questions that will help a manager or supervisor analyze any performance problem.

Can Do	Will Do
Can't Do	Won't Do

The perfect combination of these traits is that the employee *can do* the work and *will do* the work. The employee is gifted and equipped to do the work and shows a willingness to complete each task satisfactorily. If you have the *Can Do/Will Do* combination, you have no performance problems.

If an employee is not performing well enough to meet the goals management has set, apply the grid in a similar fashion. Every performance problem will fit into two categories of the grid above. Examples:

1. The employee *can do* the work, but *won't do* it.
2. The employee *can't do* the work, but *would do* it if he or she could.
3. The employee *can't do* the work, and *wouldn't do* it even if he or she could. (This is the worst combination.)

In other words, if an employee is a *can't do/will do* employee, you will choose very different interventions than if the employee is a *can do/won't do* employee. An example of a *can't do/will do* employee is a person who takes a job as a word processor and can type text well but is failing miserably because he can't create graphics, a required part of the job. In this case, an intervention might be to require that the employee complete a training course in graphics so that he can successfully perform his job and support the team as he should. On the other hand, a *can do/won't do* employee may be highly skilled in creating graphics, but she simply refuses to complete the tasks assigned. She may be lazy or insubordinate or poor at time management. Whatever the reason, she is just not doing what the manager knows she *can do*. She does not need another graphics course. She may need coaching or discipline or reward or punishment.

For almost every performance problem, the first intervention should be something called the Big Talk.

THE FIRST INTERVENTION: THE BIG TALK

Many managers have only themselves to blame when employees do not take poor performance, violation of rules, and other performance problems seriously. In such cases, the employees have never been told that the employer takes the problem seriously. Employees need to be told when a breach in conduct or slackness in some area has become a performance issue. Again, it is the employee's right to be informed of the serious implications of not changing habits or behaviors.

Many managers protest and say that they have told the employee, yet many such employees have no recollection of being informed of the consequences of their performance. Perhaps this is because managers are uncomfortable being clear and descriptive about an employee's unacceptable behavior. The most common mistake managers make is to joke with employees about behaviors that could cause serious problems if they are not corrected. The manager may joke with an employee about his absences because she is too uncomfortable to look the employee in the eye and say, "I have noticed that you are taking many days off, and absences could hurt your performance review or even lead to more serious problems."

Ironically, some managers find firing people less uncomfortable than describing their unsatisfactory work habits to them. Thousands of problems arise each year because managers skirt around performance issues. The following is a general guideline for the Big Talk. The Big Talk is the first step in defining unacceptable performance and offering solutions or consequences. It is the first line of prevention and defense against losing employees entirely. Properly delivered, it is the most effective tool for developing good performers into stellar performers.

Adapt the following conversation to your company's guidelines and policies. Review this with your human resources department to ensure that your words and actions are appropriate.

- Make sure that the conversation is dedicated to the performance problem and is not a general conversation that also includes other topics. In other words, if the problem is absenteeism, the entire conversation should be focused on the absenteeism problem. Sit down with the employee face to face, and don't minimize the seriousness of the performance problem.
- Start with an appreciation of a contribution that the employee makes to the team.
- Be sure to clearly state that the goal of the meeting is to work out a strategy *together* that will prevent this from becoming a more serious problem.
- Objectively and positively, state the impact that the performance problem has on coworkers, customers, quality assurance, productivity, and anything else that may be affected.
- Cite dates and times of incidences of the problem. Be sure to have an accurate record of these *before* setting up a meeting.
- Ask the employee for any strategies or solutions, since this problem must be resolved. Listen attentively and agree with any portion of the answer that is acceptable to you.
- Tell the employee in concrete terms what acceptable performance is.
- If this is the first meeting on this problem, you may not want to set down consequences, as this always has an ominous tone. In other cases, setting down consequences now is a good idea in case you need to terminate the employee later.

- End by telling the employee how much you appreciate his or her being open to working with you so positively.
- Expect the best, but closely monitor performance for several weeks. If the problem does not improve, follow your company's disciplinary guidelines for dealing with the employee.

STEPS TO STELLAR PERFORMANCE

The first step in solving any performance issue is diagnosing the problem, using tools like the problem analysis and the Mager model. From there, goal setting as described in Chapter 2 takes place. Finally, the most important step is to choose interventions that are appropriate for both the performance issue and the individual performer.

This book is devoted to offering you a wealth of interventions that can *turn any employee into a star performer.*

5

The Problem with a Great Employee

Are you fortunate enough to be managing a truly great employee? The temptation is to sigh, say, "My work here is done," and focus your energy and resources on more troublesome members of the team. That mistake could cost you the most valuable employee you have on board. Without significant investment in their development, great employees show a greater tendency to

- Move to another job opportunity faster
- Burn out more easily
- Take unfair advantage of the autonomy given to them because their performance is stellar
- Create resentment within the team, leading to disincentives for average employees
- Work less effectively with authority, since their skills may be superior
- Develop motivational and other productivity problems

GREAT EMPLOYEES—AT RISK FOR TURNOVER

Investing in and actively managing a great employee is a better use of your time than spending it on supporting weaker staff members. Most managers, however, pour more of their time and resources into those employees who are least likely to offer a return on the investment. The costs of recruiting, hiring, and launching a new employee, especially a great new employee, have become astronomical. The smart move is to do everything you can to keep the gems that you have, so these folks should receive not less but more of your time than the problem employees.

The war for talent is real. Yes, there are many people in the job market today, but great employees are still rare. One way to win this war for smart, motivated, reliable people is to hold on to those that you have. Rest assured, they are being approached and are vulnerable to being recruited for better-paying or perhaps more interesting job opportunities. Headhunters are calling them; their neighbors are recruiting them; old friends and former employers recognize their value. You need to consistently affirm their value and resell them on the job they have.

LOVE THE ONE YOU'RE WITH

How do you inspire great employees to value the job they have and resist other offers? Development expert Nicholas Stern says: "Create a culture of exclusivity so people will see working for a competitor as a step down."

Many great employees are great because of a personal code of excellence. They want to ally with a company, a department, and a leadership that take a similar stand for excellence. Promoting the job and the company to these stellar employees is more effective than promoting them to candidates with lower aspirations.

Several years ago, I saw this principle at work at Xerox. I was consulting with a midsize agency that supplied training programs to Fortune 500 companies. Many of the contract trainers who worked for the agency had become disgruntled. They were convinced that they were underpaid. The agency commissioned me to survey the industry and make recommendations regarding pay increases. I had the opportunity to talk to all the major companies that deployed trainers to train America's best companies in management, sales, and information systems.

I discovered something that at first made no sense. Xerox trainers were the lowest paid on my list, yet their retention rate was highest. In some cases, the agency I was working for was paying people twice the Xerox rate. And here's the kicker: Xerox trainers were considered by industry to be the best trainers out there. How did Xerox get these top performers to remain loyal and work for the company for years for compensation that was far below the industry standard?

- Pride in company
- Pride in accomplishment
- Pride in standards

I talked to some of these training stars who were working for so little, sharing with them the survey information regarding compensation. Most of them didn't care. Why? They were Xerox trainers. To them, this was the pinnacle of excellence. To be able to say that you were a Xerox trainer was a message to the industry that you were the best of the best. There were other things that they liked about Xerox, but there was one primary reason that most contractors wouldn't consider jumping ship: They would not give up the status of being able to say, "I am a Xerox trainer." A Xerox trainer had been hired through a highly selective process, had been trained rigorously, and was held to high standards of performance. Most of all, the trainers were very proud of their affiliation with Xerox, a platinum standard company at that time.

How sad it is that many employees hear the worst criticism of their company from their own managers. In contrast, leaders and managers who authentically promote their company or department as a great place to work have dramatically more productive teams that stay around longer.

But even in the best and most enlightened companies, great employees can present problems. Great employees can develop their own unique problems and deteriorate into not so great employees.

Solutions and interventions—the good news

The good news is that great employees can stay great and even get better if they are managed with insight and wisdom. There are five major areas of vulnerability that are endemic among great employees. Fortunately, managers have great interventions for each of the five major problems—all of them explored in this chapter.

GREAT EMPLOYEE PROBLEM 1: BURNOUT

When you are always the best, can always be depended upon, and always have the capability to do more complex tasks, you will be called on more than others. At first, this singling out is gratifying, a type of recognition. After a while, it just gets old.

Great employees usually become dependable and high performing through their own efforts. They push, push, push toward goals. They are always striving for excellence. They work to meet management's expectations and stretch even harder to reach personal goals. The fast track of high-achieving employees is exhilarating—but it takes its toll eventually.

At the end of the day, the great employee has expended more time and energy than most others; therefore, he or she is more drained. At the end of the week, that wearing down is cumulative. By the end of the year, the burned-out employee may be looking for another job because failure or half-heartedness is not an option. These stars often can't bring themselves to cut back or ask management for help. They may just start fresh elsewhere. Someone else's gain will be your loss. How do you stop it?

Interventions

- *Charge the employee with the responsibility for achieving balance.* Make it part of the employee's goals or professional development plan. Great employees often see life outside work as goofing off or not a high priority. Putting balance as an annual goal to work toward makes the employee more committed to leaving the office in time for recreation, family time, or other things she values.
- *Formally convey to the employee how committed you are to supporting her in achieving balance.* The first step in this process should proceed as follows:

    At the outset, state your commitment to the employee's success. For example: "Daria, your contributions to this department have been extraordinary, and your value to me as a supervisor is exceptional. I want to make sure that you are successful and fulfilled here at XYZ Company for a long time to come. You are one of the best performers here. We very much want to keep gifted employees like you. To be happy in a job for the long term, you have to have balance. I'd like to do an exercise with you that encourages balance."

Now draw a large circle, about 5 inches in diameter.

"I'm going to ask you to draw a pie chart. I'm not asking you to tell me specific personal details, but in general, we're going to look at where your time goes each week. Draw a wedge that represents the amount of time each week that you spend doing various things. For example, if you average 8 hours sleep per night, the wedge for sleep will take up one-third of the circle. The second wedge will represent your workweek, usually at least 40 hours, or almost another third. Approximately how many hours per week are you putting in currently?"

(This gives the employee an opportunity to tell you about hidden overtime, files taken home to complete, and other habits that can lead to burnout.)

"Next, draw a wedge for meals, meal prep, housework, and other routine functions outside work. Now draw a wedge for schooling, volunteer work, and part-time job hours. Then draw two more wedges—one for sports, recreation, and exercise and one for friends and family time. These two may overlap. If the exercise is done with your family, put the hours in the family wedge. The last wedge is for everything else."

(Name a few things.)

Hopefully, this exercise will encourage dialogue with the employee about burnout potential. The employee may not have complained that every week you spring a surprise project on her that keeps her there until 6:30, instead of 5:30. As she explains to you that she has only 1 hour of family time each evening, however, she can mention the problem with having to work late. When she leaves the office at 6:30, she arrives home at 7:00. Her child must be fed, bathed, and in bed by 8:00 in order to get a good night's sleep. Family time on late nights is limited and very rushed.

The following statement is very important. The employee needs to hear from you that you will cooperate in helping her achieve balance. For example: "Daria, your happiness here at XYZ Company is very important to me. I want to support you in any way I can. Although I can't say that I'll never ask you to work late again, I am committed to trying to reduce the number of times a month that this occurs." The next statement is critical. *"Is there anything else I can do that will contribute to your job satisfaction?"*

(These open-ended questions are excellent. You may be surprised at what people will tell you!)

- Recognize the employee as a total person and not just an employee. If the employee is willing to share, find out his or her
  - Talents
  - Hobbies
  - Likes and dislikes
  - Spouse's and children's (or significant other's) names
  - Accomplishments
  - Volunteer or charitable activities

  Note: Don't push or invade privacy. Some individuals aren't comfortable sharing these things at work. The safe bet is to share these things, one at a time, about yourself—briefly. Most people will then share similar information.

- *Give your employee the spotlight.* If your employee is comfortable with it, announce accomplishments outside of work in staff meetings or newsletters. "Daria Sacha finished third out of 200 runners in the Second City Marathon. Congratulations, Daria." Ask permission to share this information before proceeding.

- *Give bonus time off as a perk.* Provide flextime, formally or informally, if you have kept the employee significantly late or called him in on weekends. Also, beware of hidden overtime in the early mornings. If you consistently ask Ned to set up audiovisual equipment and tables for a meeting that starts at 8:00 A.M. every Monday, then Ned may be arriving at 7:00 A.M. If Ned's usual start time is 8:30 A.M. that adds up to at least 6 hours per month. A half day of compensatory time may be in order.

  Also, Ned will do the extra setup work with greater joy if he knows that he's being rewarded. Burnout will be deferred because job satisfaction has increased. Plus, where's Ned going to find another boss as thoughtful as you?

- *Offer job rotations to employees who have worked for you for several years.* Everyone gets bored sometimes. Call it the 7-year itch—employee style. Even great employees sometimes feel that they're in a rut and want a little change in their careers. Job rotations are a great long-term strategy, but you will make a sacrifice short term. Allowing an employee to go work in another area of the company or in another role in your department forces you to give up the employee's valued services for the short term. Most job rotations are 3 to 6 months long, and that may seem like a lot of time to sacrifice. Yet, not offering employees opportunities to try new things puts you at risk of losing the employee permanently. When job seekers fill out applications, they are often asked, what was your reason for leaving your last position? You'd be surprised at how many say, "I'd been doing the same thing for quite a while. I wanted to try something new."

- *Design a career path for the employee.* Share this in a session with your employee. Show the employee his role in your succession plan. Reveal where you project he will be in 5 years if he continues to improve.

- *Create a professional development plan for your employee, as described in Chapter 3.* Can an investment in an employee's professional development really make a difference? Consider the following example.

General William Fitts, who coordinated much of the information technology effort for the Vietnam War, never meant to make a career in the U.S. Army. As it turned out, he held every position from private to major general. He was one of those really great employees, a brilliant student, and a natural leader. After Korea, he had planned to return home to the bright future that was assured him. But the Army offered to give him time and money to earn his college degree. He stayed for that. By the time he was a college graduate, the Army was realizing a need for more MBAs in the military. Bill, as his friends call him, stayed a bit longer to take advantage of this developmental move. As he prepared to leave for the third time, Bill was approached with the greatest opportunity yet. Again, the Army recognized a need for executives who deeply understood information technology. The Army was living in the computer age but had few executive-level officers with the background to lead in this critical area. Bill was offered the opportunity to go back

The Benefits of Job Rotations

Job rotations offer many advantages:

- They keep bright and energetic employees engaged and make their work more interesting. Often great employees are also smart employees. The deadly dullness of doing the same thing month after month, *especially* if you are very good at it, can be painfully boring for quick minds. After a refreshing stint on another job, the employee may find a renewed interest in her or his duties.

- They offer new opportunities within the same department or company. After all, employees are going to leave you sometime. It's better to retain them somewhere in the organization than to lose them completely.

- They increase the employee's satisfaction with his or her current position. Going on the adventure of a job rotation may be appealing, but often the result is that employees learn to appreciate what they already have. The duties, the hours, the flexibility, and the boss at the rotational job may not be as good a fit for the employee. He returns with renewed commitment to his original job. And the next time he thinks of sending out résumés and leaving you, he'll remember that the grass is not always greener nor the work culture as laid back as it is in his present circumstances.

- They contribute to your company's being an overall fantastic place to work for the long term. When employees burn out and start putting together that list of reasons to stay and reasons to go, money is not the only thing on that list. More and more employees are looking for that rare find—the great place to work. Job rotations say to the employee, "We are investing in you. We want you to be a part of our company in a variety of roles in the future. We hope to have a prosperous and interesting future together." That type of commitment on the part of a company is very appealing to great employees in today's insecure job market. Usually, they are career builders, not job hoppers. Show them that they can find their next great job with you.

to school full time at George Washington University to earn an MS in information technology. What an intriguing area, Bill thought. He was in.

Because he valued the professional development that the Army offered him, General William Fitts served his country with energy and astuteness for over 34 years. He made tremendous improvements to the coordination of troops and other personnel through information systems. Could he have left earlier for a career in the private sector? Definitely, and he would have doubled his salary. But the developmental opportunities he could look forward to in the Army were just too appealing.

- *Great employees are usually independent lifelong learners and committed to self-improvement.* You need to support them in this area, or they may become frustrated. Offer them ideas to help them expand their strengths, talents, and career opportunities. But be ready to amend your plan. Lifelong learners often have their own ideas about what types of training and development they would choose. Collaboration is the key to making the professional development process a perk instead of a penance. Allow the employee to shape the experiences and choose the learning methods as much as possible. This goes a long way toward staving off burnout.

- *Ask the employee what she or he wants.* You may be surprised at the things that are and are not important to employees. If the employee would be happier long term with some minor concessions in scheduling or responsibilities, that's a small price to pay to retain a truly great employee. A great conversation starter is this: "If you could design the perfect job, what would it be? Tell me about it." Although this fantasy job won't be realistic, you may learn things about what makes the employee happy that can be built into the present position.

  The next question to ask is: "What parts of your present job do you like?"

  Again, you will learn what parts of the employee's current job you should reinforce and expand in order to keep the employee satisfied longer.

- *Offer variety.* Is the employee simply tired of doing the same thing 5 days a week? Experiment. Change her duties. Ask her to cross-train with a peer. Find a new role for her in your organization or a neighboring one, but alternate—one week working for you, one in the new role.

  Or change the employee's schedule. Can he work four 10-hour days and have Wednesdays free to help him recharge his burned-out batteries? Is it possible for him to leave early two days a week to take graduate courses to prepare him for a promotion?

GREAT EMPLOYEE PROBLEM 2: YOU HAVE TREATED A GREAT EMPLOYEE TOO WELL

What if you have gone too far in rewarding and making concessions for a great employee? What if the employee begins to take advantage of creative scheduling and your flexibility?

Interventions

- *Contract for change.* Even with the best employees, clear contracting is a fundamental step that must not be skipped. If you agree to allow the employee to leave early every Tuesday and Thursday to take graduate courses, state clearly that the arrangement ends when the classes are completed. You must state this aloud and in writing. One would think the temporariness of the arrangement would be obvious, but that's not always the case.
- *Avoid overrewarding.* Also, don't get in the habit of rewarding every contribution. That's a difficult cycle to maintain. Periodic rewards acknowledging several contributions work best. That practice says, "I may not reward you for each thing, but I appreciate each thing that you do." Professionals at any level do not need constant acknowledgment for doing their jobs well every day.
- *Prepare employees for positions where the reward system may not exist.* Great employees experience many rewards in the initial stages of their careers. Promotions are more frequent; pay raises are smaller, but occur often; and awards and "attaboys" proliferate. All of these rewards diminish as an employee climbs the corporate ladder. Did you know that the group that receives the fewest attaboys on the job is executives?

  As great employees flourish, management needs to develop in them greater ability to self-motivate and find satisfaction in a job well done. A great substitute for the rewards is peer support. Leaders can retain great employees longer by building strong teams that provide both a support system and strokes for accomplishment.

GREAT EMPLOYEE PROBLEM 3: GREAT EMPLOYEES CAN BE RESENTED

A great employee can make an average employee look bad by comparison. No one likes that. Without proper handling, great employees can actually have the following detrimental effects on your team:

- They provide disincentives for average, but valuable, workers who are dong their best. Implied or explicit comparisons can create feelings of low self-worth and failure. The productivity of the rest of the team can drop cven though the great employee's productivity is off the chart.
- Resentment of your regard for the great employee can create management and even disciplinary problems for you as people rebel against your authority. Teams resemble families, and a great performer's teammates will resent the attention that a star receives. The manager will be left to manage the problems that result.

The following interventions address these challenges.

Interventions

- *Try peer coaching.* Peer coaching offers the best strategy for heading off this problem early. Peer coaching is based on the unequivocal fact that every employee has a strength—somewhere. Pairing up employees to coach each other in their areas of strength builds strong teams in these ways:
  - Each employee becomes invested in his partner's success. What coach doesn't want his player to do well? Being invested in someone else's successes makes it difficult to resent that person.
  - Weaker employees come to hope that they will be the next great employee because the great employee is teaching them all her tips and habits.
  - Great employees get a rare opportunity to stretch and learn. There are fewer opportunities for development for great employees. Peer watching offers interesting and constructive instruction.

How Peer Coaching Works

Let's say you have a team of sales engineers. Your greatest team member, Kevin, a real star, is winning deals largely by writing dynamic proposals. Ron, on the other hand, has terrible writing skills. He just can't think of the things to say. Ron would rather tinker around on his computer. He's into technology and not much else. Pair them up as peer coaches. Kevin's role would be to coach Ron in how to compose brilliant sales proposals. Ron, on the other hand, can make those proposals have greater impact through the creation of tables and graphics. This graphic functionality is something that Kevin has never explored. Ron teaches Kevin how to format proposals more attractively, and both of them feel that they are making a contribution. Peer coaching makes accepting tutelage from Kevin easier for Ron. He retains his dignity, and resentment doesn't get a foothold. And there are additional benefits:

- Peer coaching is believed to be the most effective form of learning in the workplace. Think of all the things you've learned in your career from helpful coworkers who sat with you and said, "Here's how to do this." Everybody wins.
- Peer coaching is the truest team builder of all. Most team-building efforts use non-work-related activities: ropes courses, outdoor games, bowling, or just social events. Peer coaching allows team members to interact in different ways and collaborate in a more intentional and work-related way.
- Peer coaching aids in acknowledging all team members for their varied strengths.

- *Make the great employee the team leader.* In some cases, acknowledging up front that the great employee has a different role takes some of the ongoing sting out. Dotted-line leaders always have a harder time getting support than officially designated leaders.

GREAT EMPLOYEE PROBLEM 4: YOUR GREAT EMPLOYEE KNOWS MORE THAN YOU DO

Some intellectually superior or highly skilled employees find it difficult to report to someone of lesser intellect or skill. This is a fatal flaw because the management hierarchy does not always place the smarter or more skillful persons over the less skilled. Employees today often report to managers who can't perform tasks as well.

This seeming inequity is particularly true in two areas: technology and sales. These areas call for strong managers and executives. A strong IT manager may not be technically proficient. A successful sales manager may be a flop at cold calling. Their job is to manage and not to do these tasks, so in theory, their weaknesses shouldn't matter.

Over time, however, knowing that she is so much more qualified than her boss may create an attitude of resentment or disrespect in a usually great employee. If the employee does not respect the manager's authority, she may circumvent the manager—sometimes to the detriment of the team.

Interventions

- *Honestly acknowledge the employee's strengths.* Communication is the key to retaining a great employee for the long term in this situation. Ask the employee to serve as a technical expert or resource person. Do not back away from the fact that these are not your strengths. Clearly define your role. Assure the employee that you bring other strengths to the table. Stress the things that your strengths can do for him. For example: "I was chosen for this job because of my organizational skills and my ability to develop talent. What that means to you is that I plan to resolve the bottlenecks between sales and delivery. Your customers will be more satisfied, and that could mean more repeat business for you. Second, I plan to update the selling skills of every rep. Our competitors are doing multimedia presentations while we're still just handing out brochures. By year end, we'll be doing presentations that will be more impressive than our competitors'."
- *Groom your employee for your job.* Some great employees should have your job. In some cases, you should be grooming an employee to take your job—based on your expectation of taking a job one level higher. Share your plan with the employee. That will help a great employee wait around a bit more patiently.
- *Groom your employee for other jobs.* In other cases, you need to find another great job like yours for the employee. If the employee

is prepared to move on, it's better to find him a higher position in another part of the company than to lose him completely. Explain to the employee that you will mentor him and champion him as an internal candidate for the next position that affords a promotion. You will have a motivated and supportive employee in the meantime. When he leaves for another internal position, the employee will do a better job of preparing his successor than if he gives you 2 weeks' notice and goes to another company.

GREAT EMPLOYEE PROBLEM 5: GREAT EMPLOYEES CAN HAVE MOTIVATION AND MORALE PROBLEMS

Have you ever managed someone who was a really great employee, but who gradually seemed to run out of steam? Lots of things can cause motivation and morale issues, such as disappointment in compensation, lack of team synergy, or unclear direction and goals. If these problems are not addressed, they will hurt both individual and team performance. On the other hand, the following interventions will motivate and improve morale.

Interventions

- *Diagnosing the source of the problem correctly is critical.* Be aware that when great employees are no longer performing at their peak, the most common reason is that they are being managed ineffectively. Ask the employee if you can make changes or offer better support, clearer goals, or more consistency in some area. Be sure to do the diagnosis in the most nonthreatening way possible. Ask lots of open-ended questions beginning with phrases like, "Tell me about" or "Describe."
- *Chart the employee's duties.* Buy a roll of butcher paper or plain brown paper. Roll out a long sheet—at least 6 feet long. With masking tape, put the sheet horizontally on the wall, creating a drawing surface at least 6 feet wide. At the far left, put the first step in the employee's work process. If the employee processes travel expenses, the first step is that the expense report arrives via email. Write that in a box. On the far right side of the sheet of

paper, put the final step, such as "Employee Receives Expense Check." Write that in a box.

Between the starting step and the final one, ask the employee to put other boxes on the sheet to represent the interim steps that take place. Use circles to represent obstacles or things that the employee must wait for. Use forked paths and arrows to show when the process can go in two different directions. In short, ask the employee to visually depict everything about how the work flows. As the employee does this, ask her to show you where the work bogs down or frustrates her. You may learn a lot about your work process this way. You may even see a great way to solve some of the problems once the employee draws you a picture.

- *Ask the employee to develop a wish list for her job.* Again, this is a fantasy list, so not everything can be granted. Calling it a wish list encourages employees to speak up about things they might not have asked for in a real-world scenario.

SO, WHAT'S SO GREAT ABOUT A GREAT EMPLOYEE?

You may be thinking that great employees sound like a lot of work. If you are actively managing, all employees require tune-ups and maintenance if they are to perform at their peak. The great ones are worth it. And if they leave, you have a costly and perhaps lengthy process ahead of you to locate a replacement—who may not be great at all! Invest in these employees who offer the greatest payback in productivity, innovation, and contributions.

6

The Tardy Employee

Webster's defines *tardy* in three different ways: 1. late, behind time; not on time. 2. moving or acting slowly; sluggish. 3. delaying through reluctance. If an employee has a tardiness problem, the first thing to explore is which of these categories the employee fits into best.

1. Is the problem simply that the employee is running behind? Is this the only problem? Is the employee capable and physically able to arrive on time? How much of a problem is the employee's lateness to you and the department?
2. Is the employee slow or sluggish by nature? Is this a sign of underlying problems?
3. Is the employee actually "delaying through reluctance"? Is the tardiness a means of communicating hostility, job dissatisfaction, depression, or problems with authority?

The interventions for addressing these very different types of tardiness problems vary.

Creative Excuses

Today's employees can be very creative. According to the temporary place-
ment firm Accountemps, the following are actual excuses that employees
made for arriving late to work.

- The dog was asleep behind the car, and I couldn't back out of the drive-
  way.
- The line at Starbucks was out the door.
- I'm not late. I decided to change my hours to make them more con-
  venient.
- My wife and son took both cars, and when I went outside, there was
  nothing in the driveway.
- My garage door was frozen shut.
- My favorite actress just got married—I needed time alone.

These are just a few of the many lame excuses that late-to-work
employees have offered to executives. We're not talking about the employee
who on occasion runs into unforeseen circumstances. We are talking about
the employee who is habitually tardy.

SIMPLY LATE

Does the employee really have a problem? Do you?

Some employees seem to be excellent in every way but one: They
simply can't get to work or to meetings on time. The excuse may be different every time—they were stopped by a train, they had child-care problems, the alarm clock malfunctioned, and dozens of other problems that
seem to catch them unaware. The first thing a manager should do is assess
the problem's causes and effects.

When is it okay to ignore tardiness? As a manager, consider whether
ignoring the problem is an option. If you have a high performer who is
exceeding expectations in every area but this, you may want to accept this
idiosyncrasy. Under the following circumstances, a manager may want to
consider not taking action:

- Other employees are not affected.
- No services or departmental functions are unmanned or under-
  served because of the tardiness.

An employee's unique skills and experience are irreplaceable. One employee may have technology skills that would be difficult to find in the marketplace. Still another may have client relationships that could be lost or damaged if the employee were to leave—especially if he has nothing nice to say about you. Don't let an employee hold you hostage, but weigh all costs before taking a rigid stance.

Remember that some employees naively believe that tardiness is not a problem. Some come from families where everyone was always late and no one was troubled by it. Similarly, some employees come from other work cultures that did not stress punctuality. People smile about being "on Acme Company time," which means that a meeting scheduled for 2:00 won't begin until 2:15. Everyone accepts it. Moving from a culture like that to a more fast-paced environment may take some adjusting for the employee. As manager, it is your job to spell out your expectations.

Interventions

- *Deliver the Big Talk described in Chapter 4.* Adapt it to the tardiness problem.
- *Use the buddy system.* Some employees will be more accountable to their peers than to management. Find some way to leverage peer accountability. Give the employee a joint assignment with a peer. The assignment is to be performed first thing each morning. If the employee is tardy, she is letting her peer down, which can be a powerful deterrent. Be sure that no consequences come to the peer partner as a result of this arrangement. Or, ask the employee if carpooling would work for him. Being on time for a carpool may offer more incentive than being on time for work.
- *Increase the incentive to arrive first.* For example, announce that you will be providing donuts and fresh fruit before work for 1 month. The leftovers will disappear the minute work hours begin, so latecomers receive nothing.
- *Build in consequences for tardiness.* Announce that the last person to arrive will have break room clean-up duty or must lock up at day's end. Or, if appropriate, put the tardy employee in charge

of the keys to open the office or an area needed by his peers. If the employee is greeted by peers who are waiting outside the building or locked out of the copy room, he may be motivated to change his ways. If this does not work the first time, however, abandon the strategy and try something else. This is unfair to other employees, just as any tardy behavior is.

- *Offer an incentive to the group or department that racks up the fewest tardies.* This should be something fun like lunch. However, never tie peer responsibility for tardies to the buddy's performance appraisal or compensation.
- *Establish a peer coaching system.* Build into each employee's job the responsibility for coaching another employee to improve in one area. The tardy employee may coach his buddy in cold calling or mastering a new software program. The peer coach would work with the tardy employee on punctuality.
- *Be radical!* Ask the employee to be there early for meetings. On the surface, this may seem to make no sense, but it can actually be very effective. Ask the employee to come to meetings or the workplace early for any number of reasons: to cover the phones, to represent management, to wait for the audiovisual people, to greet early arrivals, to start the coffee, or to arrange the room or materials. You are then assured that the employee will be there when the meeting starts.
- *Arrange a meeting before the meeting in the same building.* Some employees who are never late for meetings with customers may think nothing of being late for internal meetings. Ask the employee to schedule a meeting with a customer or vendor or a conference call prior to the staff meeting. Or ask her to meet someone else in authority—maybe you. Be candid with the employee about the fact that this is a strategy designed to ensure her prompt arrival.
- *Ask the employee to schedule downtime just prior to meetings.* Ask him to go to the conference room and do routine reading or reviewing of information in the hour prior to the meeting. He will already be there prior to the beginning of the meeting.
- *Ask your human resources department about withholding wages*

for the time that is missed. This is not legal for all types of compensation, so be sure to check it out with HR before you implement it. Hitting an employee in the pocketbook sends a dramatic message. Be sure to warn the employee about your intention prior to docking his pay. Explain that the company cannot pay for minutes that were not actually worked. Be sure that you explain to the employee before you begin this system that making up the minutes on breaks or at day's end is not acceptable to you.

- *Withhold favorite projects or perks.* If an employee really enjoys working the phones and handling internal customers, you might temporarily assign those tasks to a coworker. Explain that customer service must be consistent, starting at 8:00 A.M. Tell the employee that you need someone whom you can count on as soon as people begin to get into their offices, and this is your solution.

- *Change the employee's hours.* If start time is 9:00 A.M. and your employee consistently comes in at 9:15, change the start time to 9:15 if that works for your department. In exchange, add 15 minutes to the end of the day. Work with your HR consultant to explore whether flextime would work well for your group. Be sure to monitor flextime closely for the first few months, however. Some employees continue to be just as tardy when their start time is 10:00 A.M. as they were when it was 8:00 A.M.

BORN TO BE LATE

Is the employee sluggish or slow by nature?

Some people are just slow. Human beings vary in many ways that can contribute to their ability or commitment to arrive on time. A person may have a greater tendency to be late because his ability to cope with the unexpected is not well developed or because her emotional intelligence is low, leading to her making unwise choices. An individual may not have the physical stamina, agility, or mental quickness to do certain tasks efficiently. Impediments like sports injuries or arthritis may be hidden handicaps. Managers can develop creative solutions to overcome some of these barriers.

Before you make any sudden decisions regarding the consequences of an employee's tardiness, be sure to examine all the reasons why the employee might be naturally slow.

Interventions

- *Work around any handicaps.* Has the employee had an illness or handicap that affects his ability to drive, dress, or do all the things it takes to arrive on time? If so, is there a way to work around that? One manager I know arranged for an employee to receive a souped-up speedy wheelchair as a gift from the company because the handicapped employee was notoriously late for meetings.
- *Look for ways to curb meticulous behavior.* Is the employee slow because she is overly cautious? Before you make a move, ask if the employee brings something to the team with her methodical ways. Again, accepting this employee as one who will never completely change is an option.
- *Look for hidden reasons for sluggishness.* Are there some underlying health, emotional, or addiction problems that may be retarding the employee's efficiency? Offer all the support you can while still operating a profitable business. Recommend a physical and offer any other help the employee may need—within reason. See Chapter 10 for related interventions.

LATE BECAUSE OF ATTITUDE PROBLEMS

Tardiness is perhaps the most popular form of passive-aggressive work behavior. Employees often practice this form of noncompliance when they grow negative. Being late after many warnings is a way for an employee to send one of the following messages:

- I'm angry with management.
- I'm sick.
- I'm depressed.
- I don't like my job.
- I don't like a recent change.

Is the tardiness a means of communicating hostility, job dissatisfaction, depression, or problems with authority? If you determine that the employee is never going to change his or her ways and that all the techniques given in this chapter still won't solve the problem, you have several options.

Interventions

- *Find out what the employee's real problem is and offer help in solving it.* Managers can solve or alleviate many of these problems through counseling, medical attention, or helping the employee to adapt.

- *Adapt the Big Talk.* In your own words, incorporate the following message into the Big Talk.

  "Daria, I feel we have been able to talk about things in the past. That is why your recent tendency to be tardy even though I have counseled you about it concerns me. Sometimes when a person runs late so much, there is an underlying reason. I know that we have had a lot of changes at work here recently that we have all had to adapt to, including me. Things at work are difficult. You may even have some nonwork difficulties that I don't know about. I am just opening the door to our communicating openly about any problems you may have that may be a barrier to your succeeding at solving the tardiness problem. That includes any problems you may be having with me that I need to know about and work on from my end. I sincerely want you to be able to succeed here. I do not want to intrude, but is there anything you want to share that could give me greater understanding of the problem so that together we can come up with a solution?"

  You cannot intrude on the employee's personal life and you are probably not a professional counselor, but you can offer some of the assistance mentioned in Chapters 18 and 19.

- *Explain to the employee that your communication style is very different from his.* Do not be critical of the employee's passive-aggressive way of expressing his unhappiness. Take a great deal of the responsibility on yourself. Say something like:

"Evan, my communication style is pretty simple and probably even blunt. Because of that, I may have missed something along the way that you have wanted to communicate to me. I want to open myself up now to really hearing about difficulties that you may be having on the job, off the job, or with me. I apologize if I have missed some cues."

After the employee replies, be very responsive to and supportive of what he says. Then, follow with something like this:

"I am glad that we are communicating like this. I know that when an employee is slow to arrive at work, it is often an indication of unhappiness. I will try to be more available, but, to be honest, I need some help from you as well. I need for you to clearly communicate any difficulties that arise in the future. Too much is at stake here for you to count on my picking up on cues every time. Too many distractions occur for me to pick up on everything. Please take me aside and tell me what the problems are or we may continue to have difficulties or even greater problems than these. Above all, I must be clear that coming in late cannot be a means of communicating to me that something is wrong. The department loses, I lose, and potentially you lose."

- Find the employee a job in another area of the company where promptness is not a necessity. Many commission sales jobs fall into that category, as do many contractors' positions.
- *Adapt the employee's job to be a telecommuting position.* The employee may be able to telecommute in the mornings or even full time.

TRY SEVERAL APPROACHES

You may need to try several approaches because tardiness is one of the most persistent performance problems and one of the hardest to change. Using a variety of approaches greatly increases your chances of successfully transforming a tardy employee into a consistently prompt one.

7

The Absent Employee

Like the tardy employee, the employee who is frequently absent can impair everyone's productivity. However, you need to be aware that employees who are absent as a result of legitimate illnesses have rights that you don't want to infringe on. Also, some employees may not share with you the fact that they are grieving over the loss of a loved one. How you handle each employee will differ depending on a number of things.

- The terms of the employee's contract
- Company absenteeism policies
- Precedents set when dealing with other employees
- Conversations and informal agreements made on the job
- Civil rights
- Best practices for your industry or area
- Legal issues
- Coverage by legislation such as the Family and Medical Leave Act or Parental Leave

Give thought to all of these factors before dealing with the absentee employee. Different organizations have different views regarding an acceptable number of absences. Find out what other managers have established as acceptable. The employee's value and track record with the company should also be considered before taking any action that might feel punitive. And to complicate the decision about what to do, some people will take sick days when their only sickness is being "sick of working." Managers must strike a balance between being compassionate and guarding the company's profitability by not rewarding malingerers.

GENERAL ABSENTEEISM

A dozen or more absences in a year certainly warrants looking into, but does a half dozen? Again, it depends on the employee, the circumstances, and the company. First, managers should adapt all the interventions for the tardy employee to the absent employee. It's also important to have policies like the following in place and to communicate those policies to all employees.

Interventions

- *Curb absenteeism with a firm policy.* The most common recommendations from HR professionals for effectively dealing with absenteeism are as follows:
  - Have a written policy that spells out consequences and issues related to absences.
  - Be sure you give these policies to every employee and clearly communicate your expectations.
  - Document every absence and make no statements that you cannot back up with documentation.
- *Include an attendance review in every performance review that you conduct.* If the employee's attendance is perfect, you have a positive point to make about performance. You also set up an expectation that attendance is considered part of performance. Employees who have regularly received a pat on the back for good attendance will understand that poor attendance will also be noted. Sometimes even good employees need to be given an incentive to return to work sooner rather than later.

COMPENSATION, INCENTIVES AND SCHEDULING

There are several ways to reward employees for not taking excessive sick days. Are you thinking that your company can't afford to institute payment for good attendance? Some companies have found that the absences cost them much more. These programs more than pay for themselves.

Interventions

According to the USA Today article "Sick Days May Hurt Your Bottom Line" by Stephanie Armour (Feb. 6, 2003), companies can use this effective new approach to curbing absenteeism.

- *Pay employees not to be absent.*

  Starmark International pays employees $100 for each unclaimed sick day. The policy allows for six sick days a year, so that's an extra $600 for perfect attendance.
      Says management: "It's worked. Everybody is aware of it and strives for it."

- *Some companies are firing employees who call in sick too often.*

  At Mercy Medical Center in Baltimore, which has more than 2000 employees, workers previously were allowed nine separate episodes of illness a year before being fired. This year, it's seven.
      The hospital, which paid $1.4 million in sick time last year, holds educational sessions on attendance policies with managers. Bosses also are encouraged to call workers who are out sick.
      It's a carrot-and-stick approach. For every 6 months of perfect attendance, workers receive $100. After a year, employees are put into a drawing for up to $3000.

WHEN ABSENTEE PROBLEMS BECOME VERY SERIOUS

Perhaps the most effective interventions are the early ones. The way you react when a problem first arises can dictate whether this is going to be a short-term problem or a long-term one. In dealing with absent employees in the early stages, a manager must find the right balance between being humane and being a pushover.

Interventions

- *Some companies give every employee a set number of days each year to use as he or she pleases.* The days must cover all sick days, vacation, holidays, and personal/medical appointments. It's amazing how people suddenly begin to schedule those appointments after work and on Saturdays in order to take a longer vacation.

- *Start a dialogue with anonymous comments.* If you are in a large office or if you have an unusually candid office, consider asking volunteers to contribute anonymously a one-paragraph example of how an employee's absence has created a bottleneck or inconvenience. Consider sharing this information with the absentee employee. Do not pressure coworkers to participate in this. Some employees, however, may be champing at the bit to unload this information.

- *The Big Talk from Chapter 4 is imperative.* Sharing your documentation of absences is part of this. Along with this documentation, bring your company's policy on absences. It doesn't have one? It needs to get one quick. You are leaving yourself vulnerable to an employee's being absent as much as he wishes with impunity.

- *If excessive absences are not confined to one employee, form a task force to explore the issue.* Make sure you include management, absentee employees, reliable employees, and all stakeholders. Ask the task force to determine common causes of absences, possible solutions, recommended consequences, and innovative ways to cope on days when many people are absent.

- *Would a part-time job work for the employee and the company?* Often, changes in a good employee's life make covering a full-time job almost impossible. Caring for aging parents or taking care of young children may make part-time work a better option for some employees. If absences are so frequent that it seems that the employee is working only part-time anyway, you might approach the employee with this option to consider.

- *Try job sharing.* Similarly, job sharing is becoming a common practice for employees who can't quite make it to a full-time job every day. With job sharing, the employee's partner can cover on days when he needs to be absent. The two employees can adjust their schedules to accommodate doctors' appointments, driving to kids' activities, travel, and other life demands. This is a win-win for everyone.

- *Change the compensation arrangement you currently have if you can legally and practically do it.* A full-time salaried employee may have no incentive to curb her absences. An employee who is on straight commission has a reason to get out of bed every day and go to work. Similarly, nonsales jobs can be redesigned to be contractor's positions. The employee gets paid when she delivers 50 processed contracts or turns in a completed audit or does something else that can be termed a deliverable. Consult your attorney before making this change, however, since you may be changing a written or implied contract with an employee.

ELDER-CARE OR CHILD-RELATED PROBLEMS AND ILLNESSES

Your compassion for a sick or grieving employee should be communicated, as should your adherence to company policies. If you have a long-time employee with great attendance who has just lost a spouse or has a newly diagnosed serious disease, show more latitude. If you have a new employee, reiterate what you can or cannot do for her according to the employee handbook. The conversation might go something like this:

"I am so sorry about the loss of your mother. If there is anything we can do, please let us know. This is exactly what our bereavement policy days are for. If you remember, we assured you that you would have up to 5 days to deal with a death in the immediate family. You do not have to be employed for a certain number of months to qualify for those days, unlike sick days. I know you have a lot on your mind, so I wanted to remind you that you automatically have these 5 days. If you need to use the entire year's worth this week, that will certainly be understandable. Do you have any idea when you will be out?"

Show compassion without letting the employee take advantage of the situation.

Interventions

- *Depending on the size of your company, consider an on-site child-care facility and a center for caring for those children who wake up with simple colds or viruses.* Similar services can be offered for elderly parents in an employee's care.
- *Pay for a local service that will handle these emergencies for your valuable employees.*
- *Sometimes a compromise works.* If an employee is allowed to go home once or twice during the day to administer medicine to older children, then he may not need to miss the entire day. Offer the employee this option, but do not encourage him to accept it or to leave children under 14 alone.
- *See Chapter 8 regarding children who call frequently with problems that are not serious.* The welfare of children is important to employees, but some of them use this excuse unfairly.
- *Pay for the employee to attend a parenting class that covers time management for working parents.*
- *Suggest that the employee talk to other employees who have successfully managed similar problems while maintaining their attendance.*
- *The key is to express condolences, but to remind the employee that there are limits to absences, even for the best reasons.* The very worst thing to do is to be so expressively compassionate that you make the employee feel comfortable about taking as much time as she wishes. Some employees won't just apply that permissiveness to this incident but will extend it to several more throughout the year. Managers should rarely feel free to say things like:
  - "Take all the time you need."
  - "Everything is covered just fine. You just take care of yourself."
  - "We'll see you when you are able."
  - "Don't worry about a thing" or "Don't worry about work."

    Those blanket statements may come back to haunt you one day.

PREVENTING ABSENTEEISM

Absenteeism is on the rise, and today's managers should be prepared to deal with this problem as soon as excessive absences are noted. The best managers will implement some of the more proactive interventions given in this chapter in order to prevent absenteeism problems from ever beginning. If you don't have this problem now, consider implementing policies to ensure great attendance in the future. The investment in a more reliable, productive workforce is worth it.

8

The Unfocused, Spacey, Chatty, or Easily Distracted Employee

Have you ever had a bright employee who had moments when he seemed totally out to lunch? Some excellent employees can have these moments. Or do you manage an employee who talks to the point of distracting others or herself from the tasks at hand? If the spacey periods or chat breaks are infrequent and don't seriously impair the work flow, I suggest you ignore them. But if the employee has lost focus or is diluting the focus of others, there are some effective steps that you can take.

CONFUSED, BOTHERED, AND BEWILDERED

Some spacey employees may be extremely bright; others, clearly, are not. Some only momentarily lose focus; others are just spacey by nature. The spaciness may be a behavior that is involuntary and impossible to change but possible to work through or adapt. If the employee's moments of seeming cluelessness are jeopardizing the reputation of your organization, consider these interventions.

⭐ *Interventions*

- *Give the employee examples of his distracted behavior and ask if he has experienced similar problems in the past.* More and more

75

very intelligent adults are discovering that they have ADD (attention deficit disorder) or ADHD (attention deficit disorder with hyperactivity.) Difficulty in focusing or tuning in may be a clue to this common problem. Employees with ADD may also experience confusion when topics or tasks are switched rapidly or have difficulty if they are asked to switch tracks mentally to deal with one customer after another.

Employees with ADD require greater structure in their work process, work space, and routine.

In a best-case scenario, your company's health insurance will pay for counseling or treatment.

Note: It is not in your area of expertise to diagnose or suggest ADD. However, asking employees a few general questions about their lack of focus may lead to their sharing this problem with you voluntarily.

- *Allow some unfocused time.* Extremely bright employees may demonstrate the types of erratic behavior just described. Brilliant minds often take off in unexpected directions. This may not be a bad thing. Innovative solutions are often by-products of getting off track now and again.

- *If possible, schedule work so that the employee has some downtime between customers.* A few minutes of quiet paperwork between customers can aid the employee in making a smoother transition from one customer to the next.

- *Build in time for the employee to think, to give her mind free rein to develop new ideas or processes, and to use her creativity for a constructive purpose.* She will have this to look forward to. Ask that she make a greater effort to discipline her energies the rest of the time, knowing that she has time built in each week to think outside the box.

- *Assign a bright employee to focus groups and brainstorming sessions.* The dynamics of collaboration will be satisfying to him. Again, tell him that the trade-off is that you expect him to stay on track at other times.

- *With a highly intelligent or creative employee, choose duties and projects that are in line with her style.* With the employee, review the tasks and projects on which she has been most productive. Try to assign more tasks and projects of these types.

- *Pair the brilliant but not-quite-on-task employee with a more disciplined employee.* The focused employee will teach his partner about discipline and help to keep her on track. The brilliant employee will show her partner how to approach problem solving or customers with a more creative approach.

- *Change the employee's position.* If, in fact, the employee is a pure and simple space cadet, moving him is often a viable solution. Occasionally, one comes across an employee whose spaciness is definitely not attributable to a brilliant mind. Once hired, these often pleasant but unfocused employees may be difficult to terminate. After all, they are there on time every day, and are going through the motions of fulfilling their duties. They are there—in a physical sense, anyway.

- *Question whether there is an underlying reason for the employee's lack of focus.* Finally, personal problems and addictions (Chapter 19) can lead to behaviors like distraction and confusion.

THE CHATTY EMPLOYEE

Some social interaction in the office is the sign of a healthy team. A quick break from an intense task leaves some employees refreshed and boosts morale. Some employees, however, take chatting with teammates too far. Since these talkative employees are usually nice and friendly, it's often difficult to confront this behavior. Managers must confront it, however, because not only are chatty employees hurting their own performance, they are hurting the performance of at least one other employee.

Interventions

- *Keep a record.* If the Big Talk from Chapter 4 has not resulted in any change in this behavior, move on to more targeted efforts. In order to streamline conversation on the job, ask the employee to use the techniques that dieters use in eliminating calories and changing habits.

    First, tell the employee that you will not ask him to change any habits for 2 weeks. All you ask is that the employee keep a list

The Importance of Early Diagnosis

At first glance, Kelly appeared quite professional and hid her spaciness. If she said very little in a meeting, she could squeak by. The problems began when people asked her questions. It became evident that the lights were on, but no one was home.

The problem, unfortunately, blew up one day in front of external customers. As regional sales manager, Kelly took her team to do a sales presentation to some of Ross Perot's top business minds. The questions from these mental sharpshooters soon exposed Kelly as being unarmed intellectually. In a fast-paced question-and-answer session, Kelly stammered, grinned silently, and said, "I don't know" countless times. The disaster worsened. It got so bad that finally, in an attempt to make light of what she didn't know (which was a lot), Kelly literally started tap dancing. Angrily, the leader from Perot's organization asked one of Kelly's subordinates to take over the presentation.

It is unfair to employees like Kelly to allow them to continue in a position in which their success is impossible. The stress Kelly lived with each day as she tried to cope with a job that was too complex for her was literally making her ill. Like most employees in this situation, however, Kelly would not resign or ask for help. She kept waiting for management to do something. Here are a few things that could have been done.

If management sees that an employee is in over her head, one option is simply to offer the employee the opportunity to step down a notch until she is ready for the position. In today's economy, many employees welcome this option as an alternative to losing a job entirely. Kelly was the quintessential "can't do" employee from the Mager model in Chapter 4. She had inflated her résumé to secure a position that exceeded her abilities. Sadly, this happens every day. Kelly would gladly have accepted a sales rep's position if she had been asked to step down. If only management had offered her that option before she and the company were disgraced.

Another option is to find a job in another area of the company that fits the employee's abilities. Kelly was great with people and could have worked in another department selling products on demand. In that type of selling, a sales rep generally has a small number of products to learn with a standard set of features to remember. That's much easier than making complex technology presentations to C-level executives. It was Kelly's own fault that she positioned herself to fail. It was also management's fault for not diagnosing her sooner as a "can't do" employee and moving her.

of any nonwork comments or conversations he has during those 2 weeks. Schedule a review of the comments. No consequences will result from the record; that is a must. A blank form such as the one shown here should be given to the employee, in multiple copies so that he can track all incidents, no matter how brief, of nonwork comments.

Date	Time	Duration	Subject of Comment or Key Words
5/26	9:15	5 (min.)	Coworker's sick child
	11:00	11	Plans for lunch
	1:00	13	Traffic at lunch
	3:00	20	Opinions of new health insurance
5/27	9:00	8	New exercise class offered to employees
	10:10	9	Employee reception to introduce vision statement
	2:00	12	Discussion of new CEO's methods and background
	4:00	18	Daughter's high school graduation

This list should include any conversations on nonwork topics other than those on breaks and during lunch hours, when employees are free to discuss anything. The list is meant to record only conversations that occur during times when the employee is paid to be focused on work.

What is the purpose of such a record? Many employees are simply unaware of how many times a day they diverge from the tasks at hand to waste time talking. Record keeping raises the employee's awareness of how much he or she is talking.

Will the employee track every conversation? Of course not. But just having the assignment will increase the employee's sensitivity to how frequently he or she starts to talk. A few times a day, most employees will start to talk and decide not to—just because they don't want to have to record it. The goal here is not a perfect list; the goal is to curb the employee's propensity to talk during productive work time.

What does a manager do with the record? Discuss it with the employee. Look for any trends or patterns that the record reveals. For example, the record given here shows that the employee tends to waste more time talking in the afternoon. Ask the employee for his ideas as to the reasons for this trend. Is he bored in the afternoons? Is he tired? Is he waiting on work from another department?

If a problem that you can help the employee with is identified, offer to do so. If not, be very positive with the employee that he has pinpointed his area of greatest lost time. Encourage him to monitor himself more closely after lunch each day. Pinpointing a time to focus on the problem is more effective than just telling the employee to talk less all day long.

Set a time in a week or two when the employee and you will get together again to discuss whether the exercise has resulted in improvement. It is up to you whether you want to continue having the employee record all extraneous conversations.

- *Ask the employee to prequalify conversations.* When management monitors excessive talking, it feels ominously like Big Brother, so don't put yourself in that position. Prequalifying should always be done by the employee. Although the employee may not be as stringent as you would be, your chances of long-term behavioral change are greatest if the employee is in charge of prequalifying her or his own conversations. Prequalifying can be as simple as a three-question test that the employee asks him- or herself before participating in a conversation with a coworker.
  - Is this conversation critical to my completing the tasks I must perform today?
  - Should this conversation take place now, or would it be just as productive if it were held at a scheduled meeting or on break?
  - If my manager were here, would she urge me to have this conversation now rather than at a later time?

If the answers to all three of these questions are yes, the employee should feel comfortable having the conversation. This may be a time-consuming practice at first, but soon the three screening questions will become second nature—taking only seconds. Review improvements in a week or two before taking any other steps. The talking habit has a way of creeping back in if the manager doesn't follow up.

- *Deal with the geography of the problem.* Sometimes, certain places become a designated zone for goofing off. Like a siren beckoning to a sailor, these spots where chatty employees congregate encourage employees to stand around and talk. The classic is the water cooler. Employee lounges and break rooms are notorious. Smoking areas and outdoor patios often tempt employees to take longer breaks than agreed upon. Smokers, especially, evoke great resentment among employees who do not smoke and who feel that smoke breaks reward smokers for a bad habit.

  What can you do? Be sure that management has a presence in these areas. No, you should not come in with a clipboard and take names, but employees should expect to see you going into and out of these areas. Management must have a presence, or problems will arise.

  Sometimes management is located on different floors from employees. Reconsider this. If moving is an option, consider moving closer to the employees you manage. If employees know that you will be passing by that water cooler or getting your coffee from the same break room, they will not view those areas as places to while away lengthy periods of time. In fact, consider moving the water coolers and soda machines to areas that will discourage lingering: near your office, en route to reception, or in other high-traffic areas.

- *If chattiness is epidemic in your office and several employees are affected, make a group activity, competition, or game of curbing chitchat.* Give every employee a roll of quarters. Buy a fishbowl and put it in a centralized area. Ask each employee to "fine" a coworker a quarter every time he or she strays to a non-task-oriented topic. Of course, this does not apply to breaks or lunch. At the end of 2 weeks, the employee who has the most quarters left in his or her roll receives all the quarters in the fishbowl.

- *Establish a vent time.* This is a weekly meeting to talk about all the nonwork topics that employees don't have time to discuss.

This could mean expanding Friday afternoon break time from 15 minutes to 25 minutes and providing sodas, or it could be a totally separate break at a different time. You may not like the idea of giving away more productive time, but you are probably losing much more than this as the situation exists now. Providing employees with time to talk demonstrates your desire to come to a solution that is sensitive to employee needs and happiness, and you will look a tad less like a villain.

- *Establish an online vent, but set strict guidelines on when it can be used.* Have each employee keep a list of topics that she or he is dying to talk about, but have the employee restrain her- or himself until a time established by management. Management then sets aside a half hour for online vent time. This half hour should preferably occur just before the end of the workday on a Friday. If employees want to stay later to vent more, it will be on their own time. Instant messaging can be used if everyone has access to it. People can announce personal triumphs, such as Junior being in the preschool play, or can get real-world recommendations from coworkers regarding work-related issues. Vents must have a few guidelines, however. See the box for suggestions.

EMPLOYEES WHO MAKE EXCESSIVE PERSONAL CALLS

All employees should have some freedom to make limited necessary personal calls. A quick check-in with the new babysitter or a call during office hours to make an appointment with a doctor is understandable. But some employees waste hours every week on personal calls. The impact on productivity is huge, and the behavior can be extremely demoralizing to hard-working employees.

Be prepared. The excuses for this productivity problem sound very good.

- "I am working the entire time I am on the phone, so I am not wasting time."
- "I can't just ignore checking on my children."
- "They called me and I couldn't get off the phone."

How to Curb Chattiness

Vents are an excellent way to train employees on which topics are work-related and which are not. Again, do not overestimate an employee's ability to make this distinction. Some really have not been trained to know when they are wasting company time. Here are some guidelines that will help make vents go smoothly.

- Employees agree to save any vent-related conversations for the weekly vent or to discuss these topics on their own time—not the company's.
- No topics or language that might be offensive to anyone in the company can be included.
- Talk about anyone inside or outside the company must be positive and constructive. Nothing can be communicated that would be uncomfortable if the person were online and reading it him- or herself.
- One person or topic cannot dominate the vent.
- State at the outset that if the vent becomes negative or fractious, it will be shut down.
- Management will be online for the vent and will recommend when a topic is too politicized for the group to include. Save those for employee lunches with best friends.

The biggest conversational time wasters on the job are topics that get rehashed over and over again during the course of the week. Lumping together all those conversations about the new lime green paint in the cafeteria gets that over with effectively in one finite online discussion. Does this topic really need to be discussed over and over again? I think not.

Interventions

- *Keeping a record and self-monitoring.* These techniques work as well for telephone talkers as for chatty employees. Adapt the techniques to recording the frequency and length of each phone call.

    Some inexpensive software will do this for you automatically. Most businesses actually already have this capability but may not realize it. Ask your information services manager or your telecommunications supplier.
- *Peer accountability can be very effective.* Ask the employee to choose a peer to keep a record of his personal calls. Each time the

affected employee makes or receives a personal call, he is to ask a peer to record the length of the call. Just this bit of accountability cures some excessive phoners. Reporting to a peer will seem less threatening and punitive than reporting to management. At the same time, the frequency of the phone calls will still be identified, and the employee will become hyperaware of the number of calls he is making.

Does this honor system work? Not with all employees, but it works well for some. Allowing the talker to choose a trusted coworker to monitor calls can have a better feel than having management monitor them. Be sure that the peer wants to take on this role, though, and don't pressure her if she seems hesitant. And never ask the partner to give you information.

- *Establish a phone allowance.* Allow the employee so many minutes a day of personal phone time. If you offer this as a bonus in addition to regular calls, some employees will appreciate your generosity. Not all will, but you will have established limits on the phone abuse.
- *Allow the employee to establish her own phone time.* In a meeting with the employee, tell her that you trust her to establish a policy for herself regarding personal calls that is fair both to her and to the company that is paying for her time. Tell the employee that since you know that she has high standards of professionalism, you are willing to try allowing her to design her own boundaries for the use of the phone. Stress that this must be a program that you both can live with and monitor, so established guidelines must exist.

Start by asking the employee how many of her calls she can make on the breaks that have been provided for that purpose. Next, have the employee make a list of all the personal phone calls she will need to make in a week. One by one, ask how long each of those phone calls will take. Add up that time. Divide that time by the five workdays. In other words, if 75 minutes of phone time is needed, give the employee a budget of 15 minutes a day for personal calls. For entry-level employees, offer an electronic timer that they can use to time their calls. This is not appropriate for higher-level employees. Enter into an agreement with the employee that she will not exceed this budget.

Revisit this topic with the employee in a week or two. Have things improved? Continue to monitor this behavior on an informal basis, since relapses are common.

- *Set a definite time for personal calls.* Again, ask the employee to list all the personal calls he must make each week. In this intervention, a specific time is scheduled for each personal call. Does the employee need to check in on children every day? Ask the employee what the best time for that call would be. Then ask for a commitment that he will make that call at that time—3:15 P.M., for example—every day. Also, agree on how long this call should last. If you come by at 3:45 P.M. and the call is still going on, another discussion should take place about the use of the employee's time. This system sets boundaries for an employee who apparently has none.

  Does the employee say that her children are calling her and that she is powerless to stop them? Give her the one check-in call home, but ask her to subtract the extra time for the additional calls from her break time. You will probably see discipline step up dramatically in that household.

- *Today's phone systems offer wonderful tracking tools. Use them.* Consider (with your HR rep's approval) getting a printout of all your employee's incoming and outgoing calls—if you own the phone service he is using and are not violating his rights in any way. Although you must be sure that you are on solid legal footing with this one, documentation can be very effective. Show the employee the number of calls and the duration. Most people will get the point.

  Circling all the calls the employee has made to a frequently dialed number can reveal to the employee the huge amount of lost time involved. Adding up all those minutes for the week, multiplying them by the employee's salary plus benefits, and then annualizing that number can produce some impressive dollar amounts. Then ask the employee to shift those calls to after work, or at least limit their number and duration.

One employer I know found out that his brokers were running up bills amounting to thousands of dollars calling 900 numbers that had nothing to do with the stocks they were selling. Only one broker had to be confronted with documentation. When the word got out, all phone abuse stopped. In extreme cases, certain numbers that are an employee's biggest time wasters can be blocked—if no one is endangered by this move and if ample notice is given.

- *Confront the employee with the cost of his lost time.* If the employee is an hourly worker, use that rate; if he is salaried, use a prorated amount of his income to show what his time on the phone is costing your company. Don't forget to count about half as much more for benefits and embedded costs.

  If incoming calls are the culprit, reconfigure the phone system to put all the employee's incoming calls through the receptionist. This is a last resort, since it is humiliating to most employees and may be expensive for you. It can be effective, since employees realize that the receptionist will know when the same person—not a customer—calls repeatedly and holds long conversations. The receptionist should be instructed to ask for the name of each person who calls and to record the number, which should be readily visible via caller I.D. Use this method only if you are willing to lose the employee, who may not be that productive in the first place.

- *Extreme solution: Change the employee's job.* In extreme cases, the many phone calls may be a sign that the employee is in the wrong position. Does this employee need more social interaction than her job provides? Consider putting the employee in a position that offers more customer contact. At the very least, the customer interaction should leave less time for unproductive personal calls.

  A second type of job change requires review with legal counsel. Consider offering the employee a part-time position. If the phone calls are certifiably excessive and relate to personal issues that are not covered by the Family Leave Act or other legislation, the employee may need to consider the possibility that a full-time position is not practical for her or him at this time.

These solutions should be considered only after other inter-ventions have been exhausted.

THE SOCIAL GADFLY

Occasionally, an employee is the self-appointed social chairman of the department. She makes a point of doing little things for coworkers' birthdays and will spend weeks preparing for the employee picnic. Charitable events give her carte blanche, she feels, to spend excessive amounts of work time raising money or coordinating volunteers. After all, it's for a good cause.

If this behavior works well for management and coworkers, then don't say a word. When the nonwork activity begins to affect productivity too much, however, it's time for an intervention.

Interventions

- *Share the wealth—and the responsibility.* Meet with the employee and tell her that her contributions in the past have been greatly appreciated. Add that it is unfair for management to expect her to do all this on her personal time and that doing it on company time is not acceptable, as it affects productivity. As a solution, tell her that you are asking that her coworkers assume some of these duties. Be specific. Tell her that Martin will do the blood drive and that Ellen will coordinate the picnic. Any other activities, like birthdays and showers, must be conducted over lunch in order to better use time. You might want to leave the employee one activity to head up, since withdrawal is likely to be painful and possibly demoralizing.
- *Establish policies regarding birthdays and other social events.* If birthdays and showers have come to mean an hour of lost time for every employee, you may need to establish some policies. Before you establish these policies, however, first determine that this lost time is truly a problem. Companies pay big money for team-building events. If an occasional cake party in the break room is helping to make your office a great place to work, you have got-ten off cheap. And cutting back on social events is probably going to make you look like Scrooge, no matter how you handle it.

If you do establish new policies, be sure you emphasize all the options that the employees do have, not what you are taking away. For example, limiting at-work birthday parties to 15 minutes is not unreasonable. A simple announcement of cake in the break room at a certain time shouldn't result in an all-afternoon gabfest. If employees want to spend more time, they can hold these parties on their own time, which is what they should be doing anyway. Employees can use their lunch hours or the time just after work if they want more time to celebrate.

- *Identify the greatest time wasters and jointly develop strategies to limit these activities.* Social gadflies will not change completely. It is in their nature to engage in a flutter of social activity, so go with it—with some built-in restraints. Ask the gadfly to make a list of all the nice things he does for the department. Ask him to put a check by any that involve phone calls, conversations, or activities during work hours. Now, ask him to identify the top three that affect work hours. Ask the gadfly to brainstorm with you some methods of executing these activities that do not affect work time as much. Ask the gadfly to consider delegating these activities or passing the baton to someone else. Suggest that some of these activities might take place during lunch or break. Focusing on the time lost on three activities feels less punitive to an employee than limiting all activities.

Whether they are distracted by social events or spacey by nature, unfocused employees will ultimately benefit from interventions that refocus them on their careers.

9

The Inappropriate Employee

Have you ever heard these responses to an employee's remarks?

- "I can't believe she said that."
- "Where did that come from?"
- "He'll say anything."
- "There's a time and a place for everything, but this was not the appropriate time or place."
- "EEEYYUUUU. Gross."
- "He's a flaming liberal."
- "She's a right-wing extremist trying to force her values on others."

Some employees say and do things that simply are not appropriate in the workplace. Almost everyone can think of an employee who behaves inappropriately. There can be many reasons for such repellent behavior:

- An upbringing that did not teach the niceties of appropriate conversational topics
- A desire to be shocking and draw attention
- An attempt to be interesting
- Self-absorption leading to insensitivity to others' feelings and reactions

- A need for dominance and to force opinions on others
- A deliberate challenge to authority or team dynamics
- A cry for help with an underlying problem such as mental illness or addiction
- The desire to establish oneself as a hero among coworkers who share similar views or language

Often, we hear that people should not do certain things in the workplace because of common courtesy. The phrase "common courtesy" is an interesting choice. Why? Because there is no code of courtesy that is common to all people of all generations and cultures. Some employees still find the use of the word *sucks* to say that something is disappointing to be offensive. However, it never occurs to employees raised on Bart Simpson that this word is inappropriate. What can a manager do to teach employees something that they probably should have learned in childhood? This one is touchy.

INAPPROPRIATE CONVERSATIONS: POLITICAL, SEXIST, PROFANE, OR GRAPHIC

A few years ago, I was training some Japanese men who were visiting the United States. They were in a multidisciplinary training program and were housed in a dormitory on a college campus along with traditional students. Needless to say, these Japanese picked up some inappropriate words that they heard being bandied about by the 18- to 22-year-old male undergraduates. The problem was that the Japanese did not know when they could get away with using bad language and when they couldn't. In one embarrassing incident, they used the worst of all expletives to the president of the college at a formal reception. It was decided that someone had to spell out for them what they could say and what they could not. I was chosen for this dubious task.

I quickly found that the trickiest part of the explanation was teaching them discernment. Why is it okay to say "darn" in public if you drop your book on your toe but not a similar expletive? Eventually, I had to read aloud to them the nastiest words in the English language and all their combinations and say, "Don't say these words."

In a way, teaching employees who are ignorant of appropriate language and conversational topics is much the same. Even for English-speaking employees, you must spell out what your culture finds offensive, because that really does change from environment to environment.

Thus, conversations that are appropriate among nurses at a hospital would not be appropriate in conference rooms. And just because an employee's conversation was not considered inappropriate in her last company doesn't mean that she will be able to make discerning choices in her new company.

Interventions

- *Be specific when giving feedback to the employee.* Give examples of what is appropriate and what is not, using exact quotes. Subtleties do not work with this employee. When you are having the Big Talk from Chapter 4 with him, you must clearly define what is appropriate and what is not.
- *Put the examples of inappropriate language in writing.* When you are dealing with an employee who says or does inappropriate things, write up a list of the comments or actions that you or other coworkers have found inappropriate. Be sure to use these examples when counseling the employee to change her behavior. Do not refer to the other employees or use their names unless they give you permission.
- *Send the employee to an offsite etiquette class or to a seminar on etiquette, diversity, or office politics—or maybe all three, as these problems are often related.* Make sure that the topics that concern you are included. What you consider fundamental may not be included in the topics covered by a particular course.
- *Discourage political conversations that offend coworkers while encouraging appropriate avenues of free speech.* The maxim "I disagree with what you are saying, but I will defend to the death your right to say it" must go doubly for managers. When counseling employees about antagonizing coworkers with their in-your-face political views, be sure not to violate their right to free speech. Suggest that in the interest of a more productive workplace and reduced conflict, they should make better choices about

where and when they express their political views. Also, if other employees are expressing mainstream views, be sure you do not counsel an employee who holds different views not to express those views. Consistent policies must apply to everyone.

- *Brainstorm with the employee about better times and places to promote his political agenda.* Ask him to evaluate the damage he is doing to his cause by offending coworkers the way he is currently doing. This nonjudgmental approach is very effective with some. The employee understands that you are not agreeing with his content, but that you are demonstrating your support and respect for him as a person. And even though you are being supportive, this is one conversation that should include legal counsel ahead of time and a witness.

- *Videotape meetings with employees' consent.* Gain permission from your employees to videotape staff meetings or focus groups for a while. If you are fortunate enough to capture the employee making inappropriate remarks on video, show her the tape. Sometimes a picture is worth more than a lengthy counseling process. *Note:* This should be done only if all employees are comfortable with the videotaping.

- *Train the employee in nonverbal communication.* Give the employee training that sensitizes him more to the reactions of others. If he has offended people repeatedly, then you must deal with the possibility that the employee just does not know how to read people. A good communications coach who deals in nonverbal communication can help. Be sure that you tell the coach that you want help for the employee in reading nonverbals rather than sending them.

  As mentioned previously, videotapes can be great aids. Play the tape of the meeting and pause the tape on people's faces as they send nonverbal signals that they are distressed or uncomfortable.

  Also, give the employee some examples of verbal signals that he may be getting and ignoring. Some employees ignore explicit statements or do not take them at face value. They think people are kidding when they tell them to stop or change the subject. Unfortunately, many people do kid around when they are uncomfortable, so they are partly to blame when a coworker doesn't take their feedback seriously. Tell the employee that he must heed comments that tell him that he is offending people, comments such as: "You can't be serious," "Let's change the subject," "I think we have covered that subject," "I don't want to hear it," "You know we don't agree on that," "Go away," or "Shut up."

- *Facilitate a meeting between coworkers who are offended and the offensive employee.* Is the crux of the problem that the offending employee is more of a problem to some employees than to others or to you? Then do a team-building meeting between the offending employee and one or two offended employees. Don't allow a bunch of employees to gang up on one person. Ask the offended employees if they want to volunteer to discuss the problem in a meeting that you will facilitate. Ask them to refrain from making accusing statements or statements demeaning the offender's character, taste, background, or other traits. Instead, ask the offended employees to start with a statement like this: "I respect your work and your work ethic. I want to ask that you avoid talking about politics in my presence, since I feel uncomfortable when you do." In other words, tell the employee to (1) validate the offensive employee for what she does right, (2) ask specifically for the desired change in respectful language, and (3) tell how the offensive conversation makes him feel. On this last component, be sure that the employee is describing his feelings and not evaluating the other person's character or judgment. Writing this statement out ahead of time and going over it is a good idea so that the conversation doesn't break down into an accusation.

EMPLOYEES WHO DATE COWORKERS

Times have changed. At one time, dating a coworker was considered taboo by almost everyone. Now that our lives revolve so much around work, this issue is up for debate. Wise professionals, however, still shy away from the practice, and you will see less of this risky behavior as you move in executive circles. Women, in particular, have learned the hard way that dating a coworker is a no-win situation. The relationship may hold a woman back or, even worse, may become baggage that she has to carry throughout a successful career. Many capable women have been falsely accused of sleeping their way to the top. One thing most professionals will agree on, however, is that the only safe way to avoid complications is not taking the risk of dating a coworker. Here are just a few of the reasons:

- Eventually, most dating relationships end. Usually at least one person is not that big a fan of the other at the end of the relationship. When an employee dates someone outside the workplace, the two can go their separate ways without having to live with constant reminders of the soured relationship. Does anyone really want to have to live with the daily discomfort of being the villain who dumped a coworker or the unpleasant reminder each day of having been the dumpee?

- Coworkers who date can polarize a department. Even adults fall prey to taking sides when conflicts erupt. Only a very naive person can think that teamwork doesn't suffer.

- Promoting one employee over the other can get sticky when everyone knows that they are a couple. One of the partners may not seek his or her full career potential because of not wanting to compete against his or her mate. Conversely, the competition can get brutal and personal.

- One or both employees may experience real pain after the breakup. It is easier to put on a brave game face and throw oneself into work if everyone at work doesn't know both partners and their history.

- A mutually consensual dating relationship may later be termed harassment by an embittered partner. Employees put themselves and the company at risk when they date a coworker. The consensual part usually boils down to one person's word against the other. Is it really worth the risk?

 ## Interventions

- *Advise an employee not to date another employee if one of the two has greater power or status within the company.* Only employees of equal status should even entertain thoughts of dating each other. And no employee who is in a position to influence the work-

In counseling an employee to avoid dating coworkers who report to him, be very objective. Make no accusations or observations if you have no proof. Consider sharing articles like the following about the costs, legal and business, that can be incurred as a result of dating on the job. Note the examples from the following excerpt from StrategicHR.com specialists in human resource issues like harassment:

> Sexual harassment may include sexual propositions, sexual innuendoes, suggestive comments, excessive flattery, questioning of a personal nature, repeated requests for dates, sexually oriented "kidding," "teasing," or "practical jokes," jokes about gender specific traits, offensive or obscene language or gestures, leering or staring, whistling or hooting, offensive or obscene printed materials, pictures, posters, cartoons, graffiti, calendars, or e-mail messages, and inappropriate physical contact or touching of a sexual nature (e.g., brushing, patting, hugging, pinching, or shoulder rubs).

> From StrategicHR.com,
> "Harassment Policy,"
> October 20, 2003.

load, compensation, or performance evaluation of another employee even indirectly should ever date that coworker. It could be a travesty if the coworker did not get a desired raise or perk during or after the relationship. If the employee did get a promotion or some type of boost to his or her career, the stigma that sleeping with the boss was a factor could follow the employee for the rest of his or her time with the company.

- *Offer a seminar or other training in sexual harassment.* Interview several vendors or consultants to find out which program most specifically addresses the employee's needs. Some highly active e-learning programs such as SimuLearn offer simulations of workplace situations. Be sure the program asks the employee to demonstrate that she can apply what she is learning.
- *Hire an executive coach or ask a senior person to mentor an employee who is behaving inappropriately on the job.* Mentoring should be aimed at the employee's total development, not just at remediating this one issue. As the employee gains confidence that

the mentor is an advocate for him in many areas of his career, he will be more willing to take the mentor's advice on conducting his dating life in a more professional manner.

- *Separate the two employees as much as possible on the job.* Try not to give two employees who are dating common goals or joint projects. That way, if things do go awry, you won't have two people on the same team who are pulling against each other. An even worse problem may arise if they don't break up: Some people find it hard to concentrate and are less productive when they are in close proximity to a lover.

- *Establish policies that are within legal parameters regarding fraternization, nepotism, and sexual conduct on the job.* With an HR consultant and your attorney, be sure you have defensible policies in writing. Document that every employee has received a copy in recent years.

- *Ask the couple if either would prefer to transfer to another department if the move would not be considered punitive in any way.* If no financial, social, or professional loss will occur, some employees may actually think that this is a good idea. Think about this one carefully, however. Some employees may feel that it violates their rights.

- *Do nothing on the job that acknowledges or makes reference to the relationship.* Although it may be tempting to kid the couple or make references to their relationship, don't do it. You may have to deal with the fallout later.

Also, for some people, half the excitement of a workplace romance is the attention that their coworkers give the couple as they fall in love right before everyone's eyes. Some coworkers may even have served as co-conspirators, matchmakers, or confidantes. Don't play into this drama. It hurts everyone's productivity.

If the relationship is known and you must work around it, ask the couple to draw up a contract with you regarding how you all will handle the problems that could potentially occur as a result of this new relationship. Tell them that you are happy for them, but that you have some natural concerns about productivity, both now and in the future if the relationship should end. Ask them for some voluntary commitments regarding how they will work together so that the relationship is not a distraction to others and themselves. Give them a week to get back to you with their list of commitments. Most employees will be harder on themselves than you would be. This removes you from being the Grinch who is not in favor of true love.

When the couple presents their commitments, consider adding any of your own that do not infringe on either employee's rights.

- *Do nothing.* Doing nothing may be the very best option here. After all, many people have met and fallen in love at work. If the couple is not violating a written policy, you may have the option of waiting this one out. The romance could fizzle away quietly, or the couple could turn out to be one of those rare ones who can work and play together to neither career's detriment.

  When relationships do end and a manager must deal with collateral damage, the first step is to open up communication with each partner privately. Meet with each person separately and ask for his or her wish list for how work and communication should be handled during the adjustment period just after the break-up. Express your desire to handle this difficult time sensitively, but with the least amount of negative impact on the work environment and productivity. Do not offer the employee any assurances that all these wishes will be granted, but ask if there is anything the worker might suggest that would make work go more smoothly and productively for a while. Since you may be dealing with people who are in an emotional state, some of these requests may be unrealistic. After the employees present their requests, respond first by telling them what you can do. Follow this with a kind and objective account of what you will not be able to do. Above all, do not show that you favor or sympathize with one employee over the other. Then revisit the previous options in light of the changed circumstances.

- *Offer company assistance to employees who need and want it.* Counseling paid for by health insurance, Employee Assistance Programs, and even company chaplains offer relief to employees who are truly suffering from the loss of a relationship.

EMPLOYEES WHO BRING INAPPROPRIATE ITEMS INTO THE WORKPLACE

Without saying a word, some employees can make coworkers uncomfortable simply by bringing items to work that would be more suitable for home:

- Decorative items that have sayings or symbols that demonstrate a lack of respect for any gender, age group, race, or other segment of the population
- Offensive or politically inflammatory posters
- Strong political statements that may antagonize coworkers
- Items that suggest drug or alcohol use, sexual innuendo, or other behaviors that are not considered professional in the workplace

Although managers want workers to be comfortable and to have some personal items in their spaces, some employees are inconsiderate and cross the line. The resulting discomfort or occasional conflict hurts productivity.

Managers must deal with overtly offensive or demeaning items, but keep in mind that employees do have a right to free speech. Rules must be applied consistently to all employees across all political lines, faiths, and lifestyles. In other words, an employee from a mainstream religion cannot display religious symbols if an employee from a small, obscure religion cannot. A manager's opinions and feelings cannot enter in as long as no one is being demeaned or distracted by the item. Objective handling of complaints is key.

Most of the interventions mentioned previously can be adapted to handle these problem employees. In addition, try the following.

Interventions

- *Put the shoe on the other foot by role playing.* First, ask your employee to role-play the situation with you. Ask the employee if he is aware that his bric-a-brac or posters make some people uncomfortable. Some employees will be astounded to know that nude plastic dolls or pictures displaying bathroom humor are not to everyone's taste. If that doesn't seem to get the job done, move on to Phase II: role playing. Ask the employee to play the role of someone who might be offended by the item. Note that I say "ask" not "tell," for this intervention must be voluntary for all concerned.

- *Another way to build empathy is to ask the offending employee to complete some statements in the persona of the offended person.* If the offensive item is racist, ask the employee to put himself in the role of a person of color. If the item demeans women, ask him to play the role of a woman, a feat in itself. Ask the employee to tell you all the unpleasant feelings that the item might evoke. Try to elicit at least six feeling words, such as *insulted, hurt, attacked, ridiculed*, or *put down*. After those words are listed on a sheet of paper, try to get the employee to continue with the role play by finishing the following statements:
  - The item makes me feel bad because _____.
  - The item brings back bad thoughts or memories of

    _____.
  - Every time I see the item, I think that the owner must be thinking about me and thinking that I am

    _____.
  - In my career, this type of item reflects an attitude that could be harmful to me in the following ways:

    _____.
  - Seeing this item affects my opinion of the owner, and I view him as _____.

    It is important that the employee come up with these attitudes himself. Ask him what he is going to do with this information. Ask him to think about it and get back to you in 2 weeks. In the meantime, ask that the employee take down anything that may conflict with your diversity, harassment, or equal opportunity policies.

Using these interventions, lead your employees to create an atmosphere of mutual support. The payoff is greater results.

10

The Unproductive Employee

Never have so many accomplished so little with so many resources as today's employees. Temptations to slack off abound as never before. There are hundreds of ways in which unmotivated employees can fritter away time and kill productivity. Some of these time-wasting pursuits are cutting-edge, such as Internet gaming or gossiping via instant messaging. Others are as old as hanging out in the break room.

In this era of doing more with a streamlined workforce, managers can't avoid dealing with low productivity for very long. Other employees won't carry slackers indefinitely, and no good manager should expect them to try. Tolerating one employee's low productivity is like admitting a virus into the workplace: Morale deteriorates, and the productivity of strong producers begins to decline. You need to stop this problem before it spreads.

HOW TO DIAGNOSE A PRODUCTIVITY PROBLEM: WHERE SHOULD A MANAGER START?

Never underestimate a person's ability to come up with a totally new way to shirk work or to slow down and reduce his or her productivity. As long as there are salaried employees, there will be new ways to be unproductive.

What can you as a manager do to stay on top of this silent but costly problem?

Interventions

- *Set benchmarks.* Which employees are very productive on a certain task? Set that as the standard. As technology or resources improve, set the standard higher. If the task becomes more complex over time, adjust the standard down a notch or two.
- *Understand how each of your employees works.* When is the employee's peak performance time? What should the employee's work routine look like?

  Years ago, a large consulting firm started each supervisory training course with a startling exercise. The instructor would ask each supervisor in the class to describe his or her responsibilities. The instructor would then say, "So, you plan, assign, and follow up on work, right?" "Yes," the supervisor would say confidently. "And you feel you have a handle on what your people are doing?" "Yes," the supervisor would always affirm. "So, what are your people doing now?" the instructor would ask.

  Each supervisor would then be asked to fill out a sheet saying what each of his or her people were doing at that moment. The task sheets were given to other consultants, who went out into the workplace to see if, in fact, the employees were doing exactly what the supervisor had planned. They rarely were.

  This was a brutal beginning to teaching the supervisors not only to plan the work, but to follow up to ensure that people were carrying out the plan. Productivity jumped following this exercise, which revealed the need for daily follow-up. Although this confrontational style is not appropriate for today's more humane and challenging workplace, at the time it was very effective. The same exercise today would probably lead to an employee filing a complaint, at the very least.

  Do you know how your employees use their time, plan their work, and manage their workflow? Would spending time exploring their work processes with them possibly lead to greater productivity? Borrow a few of the exercises suggested in this chapter.

- *Ask each employee to draw his workflow from start to finish.* Put brown paper or butcher paper on the walls. Give the employee a marker and ask him to depict every step of the process of doing his job. If he works in sales, draw boxes that start with the source of a lead and end with the customer's signing the contract or with the follow-up after the sale. Minor items like calling to schedule appointments or writing follow-up letters may be drawn as circles or clouds. Have the employee identify bottlenecks or areas where he would like more tools or training. Use this depiction to acquaint yourself with the employee's workday, habits, and ideal flow of work.
- *Partner employees who have very different strengths and weaknesses.* Give them joint deadlines or assignments. Each will contribute to the other.
- *Ask employees what they want or don't want.* Retaining good employees long-term is often as simple as asking them what it would take to help them work better and with greater satisfaction.
- *Invest in the ongoing professional development of strong employees.* Training, coaching, and mentoring should not be used just to fix problems. You can upgrade the productivity of strong employees and improve retention rates at the same time. Again, ask the employee what training she wants. Some employees see this as a reward.
- *Devote thought, time, and resources to creating or updating a professional development plan for every employee as detailed in Chapter 3.*

WASTING TIME ON THE WEB

Surfing, shopping, gaming, and emailing are just some of the ways creative employees have found to waste time at their employers' expense. On the job, employees are finding their soul mates on matchmaker.com or just fantasizing on the millions of porn sites available. They are furiously instant messaging, much of it gossiping with and about coworkers, to the detriment of the team. This problem not only hurts productivity but has cost companies millions as a result of lawsuits for everything from sexual harassment to violation of civil rights.

If you think that employee misuse of the Internet on company time is not a serious problem, consider these facts, reported by Stephanie Olsen and Lisa M. Bowman in "Office Surfers May Face Wipeout" from CNET News.com:

- Loss of productivity resulting from employees' using the Internet for personal reasons costs employers over $80 billion annually—at a conservative estimate.
- Most studies estimate that workers use the Internet for personal use approximately 2 hours per day. An estimated 10 to 40 percent of all network traffic between 9 and 5 is non-work-related. If your IT budget is $82 million and even 10 percent of it is paying for employees' personal use, you have lost over $8 million.

It is estimated that 67 to 76 percent of workers access the Internet at work for personal uses. What exactly are they doing?

- 41 percent of employees surveyed shop online at work—and some shop *every day*.
- 39 percent send personal emails.
- 34 percent play computer games, either alone or with other workers who are avoiding work.
- 17 percent are conducting job searches under their employers' noses.
- 9 percent are copying software for personal use.

As Robyn Greenspan of internetnews.com observes:

The high unemployment rate—6% for October 2003 in the United States—hasn't deterred workers from goofing off on the job. Data from Websense Inc. indicates that Internet misuse costs American corporations more than $85 billion annually in lost productivity—an increase since the year prior.

How can this much slacking off go on, and why hasn't management stopped it? Because these workers *look* so busy! We see workers in their cubicles furiously typing away, and that looks like productivity. So much legitimate work is done online that it's often hard to detect the new forms of work avoidance. In one minute, a worker can respond to an instant message from Cousin Jimmy, shoot a final bid to eBay, and be back to a legitimate work screen as the boss's footsteps approach. What's a manager to do?

Solving such a complex productivity problem requires a look not only at the worker but at the environment, the tools, and the management that affect that worker. A permanent solution will probably require a combination of tactics.

Interventions

- *Install "humane" monitors on company Internet systems.* Companies have a great deal of control over what comes over their corporate intranet/Internet. At a minimum, firewalls can be installed that won't handle the complex visuals of pornography or shopping catalogues. Monitoring software can filter out much of the non-work-related Internet activity. The more humane monitoring software is recommended, as it allows employees a limited degree of personal use. Do you really want to forbid Jill to check her personal email from her office or to zap Craig for setting up a tennis match after work? I don't think so. Monitors can filter by word or content. Some simply identify a company's biggest time-wasting sites (Sims.com, Matchmaker.com, eBay) and block those. Eliminating these biggest drains on productivity offers an immediate jump in productivity. Employees are forced to log onto their favorites at home.

  Also, when the buzz goes out that these top offenders have been removed, some employees will get the message that management is serious about curbing Internet abuse.
- *Still, another approach is to allow employees a certain amount of personal Internet usage.* After all, in the pre-Internet age, we shared a joke with a friend or passed on a bit of gossip in the hallway. Some friendly exchanges of communication on the job make for happier employees and can actually help productivity. Some coworkers commiserate and support each other daily via instant messaging. Totally blocking personal usage would block some pretty valuable communication. Go online to search for the monitoring software that achieves the degree of control that's right for your company and your unique employees.
- *Contract with the employee regarding his Internet usage.* Ask him to help you design a contract that governs his personal Internet usage. As much as possible, allow the employee to structure how much time he will be allowed for personal use of the Internet.

Amazingly, most employees are more restrictive than their managers. Other questions to ask the employee while developing the contract might be the following:

- What types of sites should you be allowed to visit?
- Which sites would it be fair to ask you to avoid in a company environment with a diverse population?
- At what times will you be accessing the Internet for personal use? May we agree to restrict your usage to these times?
- If this is the first session, no consequences need be mentioned. Consider that for a later session if the contract is breached.

- *Ask the employee to enlist an accountability partner.* If you want to avoid breathing down the employee's neck as you observe her Internet usage, give her the option of selecting an accountability partner. This is only an option and one that you should not pressure the employee to take. *The employee's rights to privacy cannot be violated.*

  State that the employee will be responsible for:
  - Choosing a coworker who will monitor her Internet usage throughout the day, usually by walking by. You, as manager, should never choose or assign an accountability partner. No employee should feel pressured to serve as an accountability partner. The role is strictly voluntary.
  - Setting up a regular weekly meeting to discuss progress and possible breaches. The coworker gives feedback only to the employee who is being monitored. It is unfair to ask a coworker to report breaches to management.
  - Setting up a meeting with management at the end of 4 weeks. The accountability partner does not attend. Since this intervention is self-directed, the discussion with management at the end is a self-assessment. Ask the employee for a detailed description of the progress she feels she's made, areas of improvement she has identified, and any help she needs from you. It's usually best to give the employee some time for further improvement.

- *Conduct a counseling session with the employee regarding his Internet usage.* Most companies can produce a complete record of each employee's emails, both personal and work-related, for a period of 1 month to 1 year. A similar history of Internet sites visited is easy to obtain. Again, be sure to check with human resources or legal counsel before proceeding. Sitting down with an employee and going over that usage is all some people need to turn their behavior around. Why?

Amazingly, some employees still don't know that Big Brother can see and record everything they do on the Internet. They may still be under the impression that instant messaging (IM) is untraceable. They are wrong. The embarrassment that some employees feel when their messages are revealed is enough to make them swear off IM on the company computer. Revealing the sites that they have visited, particularly pornographic or gambling sites, gives some employees the wake-up call they need to abandon this destructive behavior.

The counseling session should loosely follow this agenda:

1. Open with the strengths the employee has displayed in the past. Describe what you value in this employee. He will need this to support him as the brutal truth emerges later.

2. Note any objective measures of productivity loss that you have documented over the last weeks. Your comments should not be opinions. For example: "Ross, last quarter you were processing over 50 claims a week. I expected that to improve with experience. Over the last 4 weeks, however, you have averaged only 40 claims per week."

3. Ask the employee for his ideas regarding the reasons for his declining productivity. Most employees will not be forthcoming. First answers often tend to blame other circumstances and other people. Come back with questions such as: "Is there anything more?" "What else do you think could be contributing?" "What are you doing more of at work that could be cutting into your time?"

Many issues may come up, and some may be valid. Offer to follow up on those issues.

4. Bring up the usage history in a reasoned and compassionate tone of voice. Say something such as: "One factor contributing to your recent challenges in productivity, I believe, is your personal

use of the Internet. You know, Ross, I don't mind your emailing a friend once in a while or checking to see if your friend's plane is on time before you leave the office. Your usage record, however, shows that you are spending a great deal of time during the business day visiting sites that could only be for your personal use. A high percentage of your email is personal also. Here is a copy of the usage record for you."

5. Ask the employee for his thoughts or ideas for going forward.
6. Offer professional counseling or addiction treatment if the employee believes that would help. Here is a suggested way to broach the subject: "I've told you today how valuable you are to this department and to me. The pressures of work cause all of us to let off steam in different ways. I want to help you solve this and be as successful as I know you are meant to be. If counseling would help, we would like to work with you to get it. Just let me know or let Susie Thomas in HR know. Here is the card if you choose to call her confidentially. We can set something up to help you with this."
7. State that although you are documenting this session, you are confident that the problem will never recur.
8. End by thanking the employee for something he has done or a trait he has demonstrated that you appreciate. Mention an upcoming project or meeting that you can both look forward to. The tenor of these concluding moments should be forward-looking.

In short, email has offered us great opportunities for communication and efficiencies in business. Conversely, it has offered a few employees one of the most versatile tools for slacking off that business has ever seen. If you think you have no problem in this area, I urge you to monitor your employees' email for a while. You may be very surprised.

TAKING PERFECTIONISM TOO FAR: ANALYSIS PARALYSIS

Just how many times does an employee need to go over a report before it goes out? Certainly, it's admirable to look for mistakes and to consider whether all important topics have been scrutinized for weaknesses and omissions. Some employees, however, use these usually legitimate work practices to "hide out" from real work. Since this analysis and proofreading and tweaking can be grueling, what are these folks avoiding?

- Risk taking. Once an employee is comfortable with a project, she feels she knows and has dealt with its potential risks and criticism. Some employees are not eager to move on to the next opportunity, which may expose them to greater risk. New things are sometimes scary. The old familiar feels safer.
- Initiative. Some employees want to be maintenance employees, not movers and shakers. If you come to them and jump-start them with your ideas and a sketch of what you want done, they will compliantly execute what you start. But don't expect them to come looking for work. Never finishing Project A because it's being perfected is a great way to avoid doing Project B.
- Not looking smart. If an employee is spending an infinite amount of time meticulously going over a report, he may be trying to hide his lack of confidence. He may fear that if someone finds an error, that person will conclude that he is dumb, has a poor work ethic, or isn't qualified for the job. He doesn't believe that people realize that sometimes a mistake is just a mistake. Expending this much energy on polishing minute details really is dumb—and saps productivity.

Interventions

- *Restructure the work process to capitalize on the employee's strengths and bypass her weaknesses.* Do not put employees who are prone to delays in positions where they can cause bottlenecks or have a final say-so. Projects that land on their desks can sit there far too long, impeding the progress of other employees and customers.

  Place these analytical employees in roles supporting others who are better at making decisions. Often removing the responsibility for acting on the information frees up the analytical employee to move a bit faster. She does not feel the weight of everything riding on a perfectly "right" answer from her.

- *Set clear limits and deadlines in concrete terms.* This is a necessity. Define what you want from the employee in terms of how much time he should spend on a project. Set boundaries up front on how much time the employee should be allowed to invest before getting back to you with an answer. Here are some examples:
  - "Find me as many studies as you can in an hour on motor oil disposal in sandy soil. I will call you in an hour, and you can just give me what you have at that point."
  - "Between now and noon tomorrow, please tell me which three methods of bacterial clean-up you find most promising. This is just a top of mind type of discussion. All I want is your first take on the subject. I will have 30 minutes for the phone call, from 1:00 to 1:30."
  - Or, schedule 1-hour brainstorming sessions in a conference room to collect information—verbal or written. The term *brainstorming session* seems to take the pressure to come up with a finalized answer off some employees.
- *Assure overly conscientious employees that their work quality is recognized.* Give them permission to take the risk of releasing documents and projects sooner. Tell them that even if they make a mistake, the organization (and their careers) will survive. You may want to share a mistake that you made in the past. Employees who demonstrate analysis paralysis often live in fear of making a mistake.
- *Create forms or templates for final reports upon project completion.* Some employees spend the greatest amount of time composing how they will deliver their final information. They are overly cautious about their phrasing. If you create a template, you will
  - Focus the employee more effectively
  - Give him a fast, easy way to plug in his information
  - Eliminate time spent analyzing how to package information
- *Use an online project management tool.* This software tool allows your employee, you, and other stakeholders to collaborate and give input online. Project milestones are entered at the beginning of the project. If any team member gets behind, that variance is charted in a bar chart or some other visual graphic. As soon as a delay occurs,

you can see it and discuss it with the employee. This tool also encourages overly analytical or verbose employees to move on to the next step. Less time is spent filling in the information required.

PROCRASTINATION: DOWNFALL OF CREATIVE EMPLOYEES

Unfortunately, procrastination most often affects our idea people. As they creatively come up with and play with ideas, employees make some valuable contributions and observations. They also can delay getting started by staying in the idea stage, still playing around.

Mulling over ideas is only one of many reasons that employees procrastinate. For most, procrastination is simply a habit, formed when they delayed doing their homework and reinforced by nagging parents who never quite resolved the problem. Many procrastinating employees really don't mind the work—once they get into it. It's just getting into it that is an obstacle. This lifelong habit has become almost a ritual, part of the work process. One challenge that you have as a manager is to change the work process without assuming a parental, nagging role. The following interventions aid in putting the responsibility for changing procrastinating behaviors where they belong—with the employee.

Interventions

- *Set incremental deadlines instead of one final deadline.* Slicing up a looming deadline into smaller bite-size pieces is less daunting to procrastinators. You might have assigned the employee to write a business case proposing the type of PCs to be installed in branch offices all over the region. Instead of a deadline for the final business case recommending a brand of PC, try divvying the process up into mini-deadlines:
  - Please send me your short list of PC vendors that meet our criteria by May 1.
  - Select the vendor by May 8.
  - Have the rough draft completed by May 12.
  - Complete the business case by May 15.
- *Make deadlines a team responsibility.* Peer pressure is a wonderful thing. Employees who feel no compunction about letting you

down won't want to let a teammate down. Charge two or more employees with the deadline and watch how effective this is with procrastinators who are team players.

- *Allow the employee to set her own due dates.* In a planning session, state how important it is that the due date for a particular project is met. With that in mind, tell the employee you are going to allow her to set a date that she can comfortably meet. Once she commits to that date, however, she will be locked in. Once the employee sets the date, go back and question her comfort level. Ask questions like, "Will this allow you time to test for all the flaws in the program?"

    Going through this process may actually teach the employee how to schedule realistically. Some people have never been taught this process, although this type of planning seems like common sense to others. You may actually need to use this method on two or three projects before an employee begins to schedule appropriately on her own.

- *Put the procrastinating employee on the spot.* Place him in roles that kick-start his performance. Certain tasks place employees in the spotlight or in a position where failure to perform could cause them problems. This is a good thing. As manager, you want their procrastination to be their problem, not yours. How do you move the problem to their court and make it theirs? In one workplace involving trainers and instructional designers, one employee consistently failed to have her designs completed on time. The manager shifted her responsibilities to doing more presentations than designs. The employee did not want to be embarrassed, so she was always prepared to present in front of groups. Her teammates got a break from doing these chores themselves and had time to take up the slack in the design department.

    What about your employee? Is there a role you can place him in that puts pressure on him to get started and not procrastinate? Is there a role that is answerable to customers, peers, or others that will make him perform on demand? Try breaking down what your department delivers and performs. Can you assign your procrastinator to a role that gets greater scrutiny at shorter intervals?

- *Remove valid obstacles.* Does your employee have valid reasons for not starting on a timely basis? Here are some valid reasons for procrastination:
  - Necessary tools are not available or are impaired.
  - Bottlenecks have occurred in other departments or because of suppliers.
  - Direction is unclear. This is the reason for procrastination that is most often cited. Sometimes this complaint is not an excuse but an accurate description of a very real problem. Never rule out the possibility that you may be part of the problem.

  Ask your employee what are the obstacles to starting that he or she faces. Be sure you have removed the obstacles that are your responsibility. Then aid the employee in removing other barriers.

JUST PLAIN LAZY EMPLOYEES

What do you do if an employee is simply lazy? He paces himself, and that pace is definitely slow. He seems to have no sense of the amount of effort that is expected. He has no radar for looking around and seeing that he is not contributing to the same degree as his peers—or, worse, he doesn't care.

Interventions

- *First, communicate to the employee that his level of productivity is not acceptable.* Simultaneously, convey your commitment to help him solve the problem. Encourage the employee to explore whether an external factor such as health issues, personal problems, or other distractions could be impairing performance (covered more thoroughly in Chapter 19).
- *With the employee's help, pinpoint the employee's most productive time in the workday.* Shift the employee's most critical work to this time.
- *Pinpoint times when the employee is least productive.* On a daily basis, schedule tasks for this time that force the employee to perform:
  - Schedule appointments
  - Make daily runs to suppliers, the bank, or other places so that the employee keeps moving and working

- *Change the employee's locations.* If the employee becomes lethargic every afternoon between two and four o'clock, suggest that he go to the conference room and work there during those hours if it is not occupied. Surprisingly, a change of location can refocus some employees.
- *Develop work rituals.* Employees can be trained to move from task to task throughout the day, the way schoolchildren are. For example, students may know that as soon as the first bell rings in the morning, they should get out their spelling books. Work with your employee to develop daily work rituals that include things that she enjoys. For example, a manufacturing supervisor could schedule herself to
  - Complete the forecast of all materials needed for the next day and check in with three lead employees by her first break of the day at 10:00 A.M.
  - Assess the work in every bay for quality and quantity by lunch time. A form to check off for this task would increase accountability.
  - Complete all required daily paperwork by 2:30 P.M.
  - Schedule as many appointments with equipment vendors, consultants, peers, and management as possible between 2:30 and 4:00 P.M. If this is the employee's least productive time, she will be locked into activities that force her to be up and moving.
- *Explore this job and other jobs with the employee.* Is this the right job? Could this, in fact, be a problem with motivation as defined in Chapter 4?

Note: Naturally, this and other employees in this chapter are candidates for the disciplinary strategy as defined by your company's standards and human resources policies. Resort to that process when all else fails.

MAKING WORK HARDER THAN IT IS: ADDING UNNECESSARY STEPS

Some employees have a gift for creating work for themselves. They can take a 3-hour task and expand it so that it takes 3 days. Hidden messages lurk behind all the layers of tasks they invent for themselves and others to do:

- "No one works as hard as I do on this job."
- "I am the only one smart enough to see that these extra steps are needed."

Those messages are wrong on so many levels.

Interventions

- *If the forming of unnecessary task forces or focus groups becomes a habit, make the employee more accountable for this use of human capital.* For 6 months, the employee should be required to get management approval before forming these groups. Until he develops better judgment about how to use groups appropriately, someone should monitor his use of them. In lieu of management approval, two coworkers could serve as accountability partners.
- *The manager should ask several employees with projects similar to the employee's to develop a timeline depicting their project milestones from start to finish.* The employee should create one, too. The manager should meet with the employee privately to compare the progress of each project and the total time consumed. A serious talk should follow about allocation of resources, particularly that most valuable resource—time.
- *Be concrete in telling employees what you don't want them to do.* For example, "I don't want a 10-page, bound report analyzing every safety incident. A 1-page summary on the standard form will serve my purposes satisfactorily."
- *If focus groups and other collaborative bodies are important to an employee, satisfy that need by sending the employee to serve on these when someone must.* Many employees don't want this duty. Give it to the employees who enjoy it.

Many of these problems may stem from analysis paralysis. Review that section and others for more interventions.

11

The Low-Quality Employee

The employee shows up. The work gets done. The quality of that work, however, is marginal or worse. Mistakes may be so frequent that you feel it would be less work to do it yourself. Or errors may not be the problem, but the document falls short of the excellence expected by your company, your industry, your customers, or you. How do you handle the situation so that this employee's quality rises to meet the company's needs and begins to be a source of pride to the employee as well?

Employees may have several reasons for producing poor-quality products or services, including being unqualified, needing further development, or simply not achieving the quality levels that are within their reach. The interventions in this chapter are broken down for each of these three categories, but some interventions may apply to all three.

UNQUALIFIED EMPLOYEES

How do some people land jobs for which they are not qualified? A few are promoted by overly optimistic former bosses. Some lie on their résumés. Some get past recruiters who are very busy and are dealing with a competitive talent pool. However the unqualified employee came to you, that employee is your problem now. He or she may lack the skills, ability, education, or experience to be adequately qualified for the current job. Determining the way in which the employee is unqualified is the first step.

Interventions

- *Consider whether the employee has the ability to do this job under any circumstances.* Some employees may have physical or other limitations that prevent them from doing this job. You can move such a person to another position or adapt the job to the employee. Get counsel on this from an HR representative or your attorney, since any such change may be viewed by an employee as discriminatory. Under some circumstances, you will be allowed to remove employees. For example, if an employee is a piano mover, but he cannot lift more than 10 pounds because of back problems, clearly something must be done, at least until the employee's back condition heals. Can you move the employee to scheduling or dispatch? Can the employee be an appointment setter or a driver? Avoid any move that could be viewed as punitive.

- *Does the employee have a learning disability, a reading problem, an attention deficit disorder, or some other silent challenge to performance?* Encourage the employee to explore whether one of these is the cause of his quality challenges and to share the result with you if he is comfortable doing so. Urge him to use an EAP (Employee Assistance Program) or services provided by your health provider. However, don't promise that this is covered unless you have checked this out recently, as some health providers are cutting back.

- *Offer the employee an opportunity to leave on her own terms.* Employees who are underqualified occasionally welcome an honest conversation with the boss that acknowledges that the employee is in over her head. Although not everyone is appreciative of being offered a supportive exit, some employees are actually relieved. Ask the employee if she thinks she might enjoy working in a different company or industry. Make this conversation about her goals and her future. Along with the support, offer these valuable perks:

- Three appointments or 3 months with a career coach or career counseling firm
- A generous severance to help the employee get started elsewhere
- A professionally produced résumé, paid for by the company
- Any career transition services that your company offers

- *Reconfigure the job to avoid tasks that the employee cannot do.* These impossible tasks can be avoided in many ways:
  - Job sharing. With part-time employees, you can take one job and make it into two jobs. For example, if you are an accountant and you have part-timers helping you during tax season, you may find an employee who is great at gathering information from customers, but who makes many mathematical errors. This employee can share a position with an employee who is an expert number cruncher but who may not be as effective at meeting the public. Sometimes two employees together can make up the perfect employee. Use the strengths of each.
  - Trade responsibilities among staff so that everyone is doing tasks that he or she can accomplish competently. Again, be sure the changes do not penalize other employees.
  - Change the employee to part-time. Use the savings from his pay reduction to hire a temp or another part-timer to do the tasks that this employee can't perform.

EMPLOYEES WHO ARE CAPABLE OF BEING AMAZING BUT WHO SETTLE FOR AVERAGE

An employee who is capable of dazzling performance but who achieves only average results is as much a waste as an unqualified employee. Organizations can afford to accept average performers who are achieving average results. Accepting mediocre results from an employee with outstanding abilities is throwing away a valuable resource, human capital. A manager who does this is doing both the employee and organization a disservice. There are several steps to resolving this fairly common problem.

Interventions

- *Give the employee a vivid picture of what you want.* What does "good" performance look like? When you explain your performance standards to your employee, spell out your criteria, such as the acceptable number of mistakes and quantity and quality requirements, using lots of examples. Do you manage a proposal writer who turns out mediocre but not bad proposals? Show her three examples of great proposals along with your explanation of why they are good. Then show her three examples of poor or mediocre proposals and tell her what they lack. Amazingly, some employees don't know what "good" performance looks like. It is your job to show them.

  In addition, every task should have quality standards. In the example of the proposal writer, whose responsibility is it to proofread? What are the approved format, dimensions, and content of proposals? Spell this out and give it to employees in writing. Similarly, create a list of signs of poor quality. Employees should know what not to do. Many employees think that no one cares if spelling in emails is incorrect. Their management, on the other hand, may be horrified at this lapse in professionalism. Spell out what is not acceptable.

- *Discover the reason why the employee is choosing mediocrity.* What if you have verified that the employee is capable of doing a high-quality job but simply won't do it? This is an entirely different problem. Pinpoint with the employee exactly what elements of the job he finds problematic and then work around them. Is there a part of the job that is repugnant to him or that he considers beneath his level of experience? Or is this a personal issue? Is his noncompliance with quality standards the employee's way of expressing resentment toward another employee or toward you? Ask the employee to list everything he likes about the tasks he does and then list the things he does not like. Ask him how many minutes or hours a day he spends doing the repugnant tasks. Point out that every job has some unpleasant parts. Underscore to the employee that you are searching for a solution to a quality problem that unequivocally must be solved immediately. Stress, however, that you are trying to work toward the employee's success and satisfaction at the same time. Enlist the employee's help in figuring out a solution to this mystery. If possible, reach some compromises. Together, attempt to create some solutions, but give the employee a deadline for improving his quality. Check in to make sure that the solutions are being implemented.

- *Participate in team-building or relationship-building exercises with this employee if her issue is personal and not professional.* With an outside consultant or on your own using off-the-shelf or online programs, try to work through the rebellion that the employee is demonstrating. The American Management Association or the American Society of Training and Development can offer you a variety of games and job aids aimed at improving the dynamics of your relationships. Some are as simple as answering a series of questions so that you and the employee get to know each other better. Others are designed to reveal your different personality styles to each other and to increase tolerance for different styles. Some courses, like ropes courses, have you engage in a fun activity designed to increase your trust in each other and to create a bonding experience.

- *Ask the employee to present his work to his peers or to management and let the embarrassment be his.* If the risk to you is not great, allow the employee to present his shoddy work to his peers or to management. If he is capable of better, he will probably be embarrassed. The embarrassment about his work should be not yours but his. This intervention works only if the employee knows that he will be responsible for presenting this work to others and doesn't want to look ill-prepared or unprofessional in front of others.

- *Ask the employee to train or mentor others.* This may sound contradictory if the employee's work has not been a model of excellence in the past. The best way I know to learn to be better at something, however, is to teach it to others. That forces a bored employee to tune in and pay attention to details. Watch the employee closely, however. Although this usually works, you need to watch to make sure that the employee is not teaching others her slovenly ways.

- *Show the employee dramatic results of poor quality.* If the employee's inferior quality can lead to safety issues or material damage, try to find photos or videos of the results of mistakes and poor quality. Much of this can be found online now. Ask the employee to research and write a report or a list of all the ways in which poor quality could hurt the company, customers, the department, and him.

- *Devise a quality checklist.* With this device, employees must check for quality and sign their names to verify that quality meets standards.

- *Use the buddy system, so that employees encourage one another to complete their work with excellence and on time.* Some employees who don't do well as individual contributors are great team players. Use peer pressure to get them to do their work well and promptly. Ask buddies to use the quality checklist just mentioned to verify quality.

- *Remember that a dip in quality can be a cry for help.* Has the employee become depressed or addicted, or does she simply need to talk? Employees may allow quality to suffer in order to start a dialogue with management. Changes in quality are classic workplace symptoms of serious psychological or even health problems. Chapter 19 offers more interventions for this type of problem.

- *Build in and enforce consequences.* Some employees will never respond to words or threats or subtleties. They must feel the consequences personally or they will never work toward upgrading quality. At first, the low quality is your problem. You must find a creative way to make it the employee's problem. For example, if the employee is part-time and wants to work more hours, give more hours to coworkers whose work quality is higher. Be sure that you do not violate any agreements you have with the employee. Tell the employee that you are awarding more hours for superior quality.

- *Allow a full-time employee whose work is superior to work on the more interesting and prestigious projects.* Be sure the employee who does poor-quality work knows that you are doing this intentionally.
- *Create an elite team that works on a few coveted projects.* Make consistent quality a criterion for getting on the team. Do employees like projects that get them out of the office? Then announce that the traveling team will include only those employees with the fewest errors.
- *Award cash or prizes for consistent quality over a short period of time.* Money talks. Or take the achievers of highest quality to lunch each Thursday in June.
- *Give the gift of time.* Allow employees whose work is complete and error-free to leave 1 hour early on Friday or to take a 2-hour lunch on Wednesdays.
- *Look to the future.* Is the employee aware that his lack of quality can block future opportunities for promotions and raises? As manager, it's your responsibility to make explicit these rather obvious realities that the employee may be in denial about. Have an intentional conversation with the employee explaining how achieving high-quality standards relates to his future.

EMPLOYEES WHO NEED FURTHER DEVELOPMENT AND TRAINING

Sometimes an employee needs further training in order to fulfill her or his job duties. The employee may have performed well in the past, but a change in duties may be too challenging for her or him, given her or his current skill set. An investment in developing and training an employee is one of the best investments that a company can make.

Interventions

- *Look at the employee's tools and work environment.* Would having a printer close by improve the employee's quality and time management? Is the lighting so poor that checking work is difficult? Does the employee have ample space to do necessary work and quality checks? Make necessary changes or purchase resources that are reasonably supportive of better quality.

- *Use shadowing to determine any specific training or development needs*. Work alongside the employee to assess areas in which he needs coaching or counseling. Or, ask an employee who has performed the same job successfully to shadow the challenged employee for a day or up to a week. When you find the skills that the employee needs to perfect, use a variety of developmental interventions, including
  - Vendor training
  - Outside training, such as workshops
  - One-on-one training
  - Peer coaches or expert tutors
  - Online learning
  - Intracompany training
- *Do a 360° evaluation*. In this procedure, peers, subordinates, management, and the employee evaluate the employee's performance using an approved and standardized tool. Guard everyone's privacy during this process. This valuable tool often brings to the surface problems that have held an employee back for a long time. Contact human resources or organizational development Web sites or consultants to find the appropriate version of this tool. If the employee is open to constructive feedback and will work toward positive change, this can be a great process.
- *Assess the employee's work habits*. Does the employee have any work habits that are stealing time from her performance and diluting attention to quality? Is longing for a cigarette break distracting the employee several times a day? Is an ill-planned workflow sending the employee to the copier room too many times a day? Would fewer trips allow greater concentration on detail? Does the employee stop work to chat during her most productive times? Does the employee's flextime cause her to leave too early each day to do a final quality check?

Quality of work issues have been the focal point of the greatest investment of time and money by businesses of the twentieth century. If you are struggling with these issues, do not feel that this is a problem that is peculiar to your company or department. Companies are forever looking for new programs that magically boost quality across the board. ISO 9000 and Total Quality Management are just two of the major initiatives focused on upgrading quality throughput and services. Dealing with the individual whose quality is substandard is the most effective approach to solving greater problems. Quality issues are solved one employee at a time.

12

The Shy or Uncommunicative Employee

Employees may hold back communication for a variety of reasons:
- A lifelong habit of shyness
- Fear of assertiveness
- Overanalyzing what to say and letting opportunities to speak pass them by
- Fear of reprisal, rejection by management or peers, or looking foolish
- Keeping resentful or critical thoughts bottled up
- Being endowed with the rare and wonderful quality of listening, but failing to show it by responding

Some reasons for an employee to appear shy and quiet are actually rooted in some valuable traits. If the employee is a great listener, he or she will be an excellent contributor long term and an asset to any team. Still, the employee needs to learn to be more responsive in the short term so that others will not mistake his or her quietness for apathy or hostility. Coworkers may perceive shy employees as poor contributors to team projects, simply because they are slow to warm up and offer comments.

SHY IN MEETINGS

Employees who are shy in meetings deprive the team of ideas and expertise that could contribute to the team's success. This problem is compounded when shy employees later confide to others that they had a better idea or that they silently disagreed with some of the ideas brought forth in the meeting. Shyness is a problem that deserves compassion, but some people have allowed themselves to avoid contributing by hiding behind that shyness. Like any other developmental need, shyness should be addressed with interventions.

Interventions

- *Assign the employee a role in the meeting at first, and gradually lead up to voluntary participation.* Do you have an employee who won't participate in meetings? Ask the employee to break his pattern of silence by reading the minutes of the last meeting or by announcing a company dinner or some other noncontroversial item. At the next meeting, gradually increase the employee's participation. Ask him to do something interactive, such as asking for a show of hands on a topic or passing out a handout. Before another meeting, tell the employee that his only assignment is to express one opinion or make one unsolicited comment. Sometimes breaking the ice is all it takes. Once these reticent employees have the experience of speaking up, they often continue to be strong contributors without long-term prompting. They may simply need to see that their comments will be valued and listened to by their peers and by management. After a couple of successful experiences, you may not be able to stop them!

- *If an employee doesn't contribute in meetings because of apathy or laziness, ask her to prepare for meetings and require her to make at least one contribution per meeting.* Offer to coach the employee in how to become a stronger contributor to team meetings. To aid the employee in preparing for meetings, give her a copy of the agenda or proposed topics. Then ask the employee to write two or three sentences giving her thoughts, opinions, and suggestions regarding each topic. Require her to turn these in to you before meetings and coach her in how to form suggestions based on what she has written. Do this for two or three meetings.

- *Ask the employee to lead a meeting.* After taking some of these preliminary steps, ask the employee to lead a meeting. Help him be successful by aiding him in preparation, but once you and he are in the meeting, do not take over.

- *If the employee is hesitant to be assertive, consider assertiveness training.* Prior to that, however, take the time to tell the employee how entitled she is to assert her opinions and objections. Offer your support, and encourage the employee to speak up in the next meeting.

SHY WITH TEAMMATES

Working together is very much like learning to dance together. The more exposure to being close you have and the more practice you give it, the more smoothly you can read each other's cues and signals. Soon your performance will be dynamic and in sync.

Interventions

- *An employee who is shy with teammates should be placed in controlled, low-risk situations that require participation, starting with a single partner.* Many projects can be done with a partner. Pair the shy employee with a teammate whose personality and temperament would seem to be a good match. Avoid impatient or perfectionist employees for this pairing. Start the pair with a very brief (one day or less) project, if possible. That takes a lot of pressure off both employees. The first project should be low-stress and may even seem like busywork. The point is to make the shy employee more comfortable interacting with teammates. Gradually build up to longer projects. Next, pair the employee with a different teammate, or even with two or more in a group.

- *Conduct team-building exercises, play games together, do an outdoor retreat, or ask a consultant to lead you through trust-building or communication exercises.* There are many things that you and your team can do together to get to know one another so that you will work in tandem more productively. One manager I know takes her team out to dinner and to a concert once a year. Her team is not particularly athletic, and this works well for everyone on it. Spouses are invited, which aids some of the shy employees in being more social.

- *Employees who don't bring up problems readily may need job aids or structured avenues to encourage them to be candid.* For example, the old suggestion box is a job aid to encourage shy employees to offer ideas or suggestions. You can start an online suggestion list and discuss the topics placed on it at regular staff meetings.

  Here is one stimulating exercise that works if you have a staff of at least five. Ask each person to name the person he or she is most dependent on in getting work out the door each week. The ensuing conversation may surprise you. The next question to the staff is, "What do you need from each person around this table?"

- *Conduct 360° assessments of all teammates and identify areas of need.* These assessments ask an employee's peers, subordinates, the employee himself and management to rate the employee on all kinds of traits and performance issues. Although these should be done anonymously, you can open the floor in a meeting for people to voluntarily state one or more strengths and weaknesses. Fellow employees can then offer suggestions for developing areas of weakness. There may be a little defensiveness, and maybe even some fireworks, but this is better than allowing an employee to keep resentments bottled up inside for too long.

- *Assign the shy employee a mentor or peer coach.* Ask another employee to work with the shy employee on a skill, which doesn't have to be communication. Working with another employee on any skill can begin to make the shy employee more comfortable, since she feels that she has an ally or a friend on the team.

SHY WITH MANAGEMENT

This employee cannot talk comfortably with you. Perhaps the employee cannot maintain eye contact or may simply get nervous or avoid you. These are just some of the clues that an employee is very shy around you because you supervise or manage him or her. Some employees are very comfortable around peers but suddenly become shy around superiors. Often this is rooted in an upbringing that stressed respect for, or even fear of, authority. A little of this respect is a good thing. Too much blocks healthy communication between manager and employee. The following interventions will open up those vital communication lines.

Interventions

- *Be creative in giving the shy employee more control.* Overly sensitive employees may need to feel more in control of the mode of communication in order to handle the communication well. Do you need to communicate with the employee about something that you think he may be overly sensitive about? Ask him if he wants to choose a different location for the talk. If you usually meet in your office, would he prefer to walk to the cafeteria with you and have coffee? After you discuss the issue, would he like the option of responding by email and agreeing to discuss the email with you at a later time? Offering to put the employee in his comfort zone goes a long way toward calming some very sensitive people.

- *Ask the employee to tell you about the greatest relationship she has ever had with a boss.* Make mental notes as she talks about what that boss did that made the employee open up. Summarize the information for the employee: "So you liked Don Watson's way of talking about projects to you ahead of time and allowing you to brainstorm before you had to offer an opinion. I would like to try doing that more. In addition to that, what else can I do to improve your comfort level when you are communicating with me?" In time, your sincere attempt to work through this shyness problem should work. If it doesn't, consider that the shyness may be an avoidance technique. In that case, see Chapters 11, 15, and 16.

SHY WITH CLIENTS

Some people are great with coworkers, but meeting clients for the first time throws them into a panic. This type of shyness cannot be indulged, as it can be costly for a company. Many of the interventions given earlier in this chapter work in this situation, but there are additional ones that relate to this specific problem.

Interventions

- *Give shy people props, scripts, demos, or whatever crutches will make them successful if they are required to call on customers.* Props are amazing cures for shyness in some people. Shyness is, in part, a form of too much concentration on self: "How am I being perceived?" "What if I say the wrong thing?" "What are they thinking about me?" When an employee walks into a customer's door or into a meeting with a prop, the employee's focus is shifted to that prop. Do you have a scale model of a machine you are selling? If you are selling cleaning chemicals, do you have a before and after sample on a board? Is there a trap on your water sewage equipment that filters out debris that could lead to repairs? The equipment may be too large to haul around, but the employee can bring the tiny trap. Demos work just as well. Be creative. Think of something that the employee can bring to talk about so that he won't be so concerned about himself.
- *Offer to write out for her a script or presentation that you have found successful.* She may not follow it exactly, but she may feel more empowered if she is using a script that has been successful for someone else. Scripts can be used with customers, in meetings, on the phone, and in many other situations.
- *If this is feasible, send the employee out with a partner the first time he meets with a client.* Some sales departments have enough depth to send two salespeople out on a first call. In other situations, a technical person who is supporting the sale may go.
- *Reevaluate the employee's fit with this position.* If the shyness is a source of great discomfort to the employee or if the shyness is hurting profitability, consider shifting the employee to another position.

SHY ON THE PHONE

An employee who can carry on a perfectly pleasant conversation in person may suddenly lose all his or her interpersonal skills on the phone.

What causes this phenomenon? First, the employee may come from a home in which the telephone was used strictly for conveying necessary information. In the 1950s, some communities still had a lot of party lines. Some families with these lines developed very abrupt styles on the telephone in order to keep the line clear and to be considerate of others. Those individuals often passed their style on to their children, who may now work for you. In other cases, a person may feel frustrated because he is most expressive with his face and body language. The telephone hampers his style and is not comfortable. There are many reasons for a person to avoid saying much on the phone. For every such employee, however, there is an intervention.

Interventions

- *In many cases, the employee is not aware that his style is terse or stand-offish.* Simply describing the employee's behavior using a couple of examples may be all it takes to see a remarkable change. Although the employee will probably be stunned to know that his style is so different from the norm, awareness of this may effect an immediate change. Be sure to convey your constructive criticism sensitively.
- *Role-play a couple of typical workplace phone conversations with the employee.* Tell her ways in which she can be more conversant and positive.
- *Telephone skills classes and videos offer great modeling of correct style.* See the American Management Association's list of offerings.

Shy or uncommunicative employees can make tremendous contributions if they are managed effectively. Explore ways to bring out these often insightful employees, and develop an appreciation for their communication style. Pause to consider the parts of this quiet employee's personality that are beneficial to the employee and to your team. Then implement interventions that will strengthen the shy employee and the team simultaneously.

13

The Overpowering Employee

Some employees bulldoze over other employees, obnoxiously pushing forward their opinions and agendas while leaving little room for the ideas of others. They don't listen and they don't take direction well, and this can lead to authority and discipline problems. Employees may demonstrate this overpowering behavior in several ways:

- Dominating meetings
- Dominating conversations
- Pushing agendas too aggressively

What can you do besides sending the employee's mother a nasty letter for not teaching him or her to share and play nicely with others? The following interventions should help.

DOMINATING MEETINGS

This employee is the dominator. If he doesn't have the floor, he steals it. Once he has it, he holds forth for far too long. He may have a dismissive way of brushing aside the ideas of others, since he is so focused on his own ideas. The dominator must be stopped by an intervention because he will never have the sensitivity to stop himself.

Interventions

- *If the overpowering employee's talking too much in meetings is a problem, enlist the employee's help to encourage a shy coworker to participate more.* Tell the employee that as part of employee development, you are asking a less vocal coworker to speak up more in meetings. Ask the talkative employee to talk only when absolutely necessary in order to put pressure on the quiet employee to contribute.
- *Ask the employee to write down her thoughts during the meeting instead of verbalizing all of them.* Later, she can edit them, perhaps with your guidance, and share by email what she had wanted to hold forth on in the meeting. Sometimes this follow-up is so much trouble for the employee that the sharing is never done. In some cases, that's just fine.
- *Give the employee specific boundaries regarding how many times and how long he can speak in meetings.* For example, tell the employee that he can speak only twice in a meeting and for no more than 3 minutes each time. You may want to offer him a reward for doing this in one or two meetings.
- *An employee who does not listen well to her teammates' ideas should be required to take notes as her teammates talk.* The employee should then summarize what she thinks their key points were and verify her understanding of these points with her teammates. The verification step must be done before any different ideas or challenges can be brought up. Just listening for understanding and checking in with teammates can sometimes slow down an employee's tendency to overpower a conversation.
- *If one employee monopolizes meeting time, develop a meeting format that does not allow excessive talking.* One method is to place all presentations by teammates first on the agenda, followed by items that are not open for discussion. Announce at the beginning of the meeting that you will not be stopping for discussion during presentations. All comments or ideas should be held until the end of the

meeting. Then allow very little time for discussion at the end. I once was in a group that did not allow anyone to make a second comment until every member had participated at least once. That put pressure on shy people to speak up, but it also stymied loquacious employees who would otherwise have monopolized the conversation.

- *In meetings with obnoxious or intimidating folks, walk over and stand very close to them.* Some employees are looking for attention, and this seems to satisfy this need. Others may simply be made uncomfortable by this closeness and grow quieter. For whatever reasons, close physical proximity of a speaker or manager tends to subdue some obnoxious employees.

- *Structure, structure, structure is what some overpowering employees need.* For a given period, structure how meetings are held, how ideas are solicited, and other forms of group communication. During presentations, have departmental rules about how many comments can be made by one person and veto interruptions. Providing guidelines may give the overpowering employee the boundaries he is seeking. Be sure to present this as a means for drawing out communication from more employees. If you do not share your reasons, even good employees may find these rules punitive. Use common sense, and if these rules prove to be too restrictive, change your mind. After all, you did not say that you planned to monitor participation forever. However, if the structure works well for most employees, you may want to keep the new format.

DOMINATING CONVERSATIONS

Conversation is even more difficult to manage than meetings if you have a dominating employee. To some degree, you must depend on the cooperation of your team and the dominator him- or herself. For healthy communication and to build supportive long-term team relationships, apply the appropriate interventions while this problem is in its early stages.

Interventions

- *Pair a timid employee with a dominant one, but have them switch roles on a project.* In a meeting with both employees, tell them that Jerry (the timid employee) will be the leader and that George (the dominating employee) will be his assistant on a short-term project. George can submit ideas, but Jerry is to be the decision maker. Ask George to do research and legwork as directed by Jerry. Make it clear that the final presentation will be done by Jerry, and that you are charging George with making him success-ful. Your validation of Jerry's role should increase his confidence and his ability to speak up to George.

- *Do personality or communication style surveys to identify the var-ious personality styles on your team.* Carl Jung began an approach to communicating that helps employees appreciate and work more effectively with people who have personalities quite different from their own. Today, many companies, including Myers-Briggs, Gary Smalley, and Drake, Beam, Moran, offer assessment tools that help each employee on a team recognize his or her unique personality or communication style and how to adapt it to coworkers. The result? After processing through the assessments with a trainer, the methodical, analytical employee usually works more efficiently and happily with the free-spirited, creative thinkers; and the blunt, all-business, driving personalities seem to develop more appreciation for the more relationally focused employees who previously seemed to be wasting time on touchy-feely things.

    With a qualified facilitator, work through exercises that teach all employees how to value and work effectively with a strong or passive or any other type of personality style. Build trust within your team through the exploration of the idiosyncrasies of each of the four major personality styles. Productivity and mutual support will increase as these exercises reveal that people are hard-wired to be pushy or passive and are not necessarily trying to be difficult.

- *Suggest that the overpowering employee has served in a leader-ship role in the past (and will do so in the future), so you want a shyer employee to have this developmental opportunity.* The key here is that management should treat the overpowering employee with respect throughout this process. This role reversal may be painful for him and may raise questions about job security, future promotions, and other major issues. Handle both employees sensitively and communicate on all these issues.

- *Give talkative employees communication skills training or coaching on script writing, interrupting, clipping, and other offensive conversation habits.* Script writing is the habit of writing a mental script of what you will say next while someone is trying to talk with you. If you have your comment ready to go as soon as the first word is out of the other person's mouth, she knows that you have not been listening, but instead have been thinking of what you are going to say. That leads to clipping, which is commenting so soon that the other person feels cut off—even when you haven't blatantly interrupted. A course in listening would probably be most valuable for employees who engage in these practices. Sources for such courses include the American Management Association, the American Society for Training and Development, and any large corporate training department.

PUSHING AGENDAS AND PEOPLE TOO AGGRESSIVELY

Everyone thinks that his or her ideas are the best. Healthy assertion is a good thing. Aggression is not. Some employees become almost driven to force others to agree with them and to support their ideas and projects. If interventions are not implemented, some employees will become discouraged and may give in to an aggressive employee simply because of the intensity of the aggression. That does not lead to a balanced workplace. Take action.

Interventions

- *Employees who are bossy or dominating can sometimes gain self-awareness by role playing the role of a peer.* Ask the bossy employee to play the role of a quiet or timid coworker. You play the role of the bossy employee, boldly stating your agenda and opinions and replaying conversations similar to those that have taken place in the past. As you role-play, ask the so-called timid coworker how he feels about what you are saying and doing. By putting the bossy employee in his coworker's position, you may show him how unpleasant his behavior is.

If a coworker's irritation with the bossy employee is common knowledge, you may ask the coworker to do the role-play instead of you. This can be volatile, so ask yourself whether you want to risk inflaming an existing problem. Be careful to monitor this and to get both parties to agree to stop if emotions run too high. Though not always pleasant, this exercise can build sympathy and awareness.

- *Ask the bossy employee to write a letter as if it were being written by a coworker who has been the victim of her intimidation.* The letter should be written as if the intimidated employee were writing to a close friend or cousin about what is going on at work. In the letter, the coworker should describe what he does and does not like about the bossy employee and give some examples.

- *Take away anything that may be reinforcing the dominating or intimidating behavior.* Sometimes bossy employees push their agendas because that tactic has been successful in the past. Don't reward this type of behavior by giving in, if possible. If the employee interrupts or talks over a quieter employee, continue to focus on the quieter employee and don't acknowledge the interrupter. Sadly, when a manager complains about an employee like this, the manager may be unconsciously rewarding and reinforcing the repugnant behavior.

- *Give the employee a place to push his agenda.* Employees who push their agendas on others and mow down alternative options can make the workplace uncomfortable. Schedule two separate meetings. The second meeting should be for the pushy employee to state his agenda. The first should be for another employee to express her view of what should happen, and in this meeting no rebuttal, criticism, or challenges from the pushy employee are permitted. Separating the two meetings provides a better opportunity for the pushy employee to listen, since he is under no pressure to develop his rebuttal on the spot.

- *Confront the employee if she is using other employees to push her agenda.* Controlling employees try to push their agendas in quieter, more relentless ways. Bring those agendas to the surface and address them one-on-one with the employee. Say something like, "Evie, I've heard that you think we should move our annual conference to an offsite location. I'd like to hear your thoughts about why you think that would be preferable to what we have done in the past. Do you want to meet tomorrow at 2:00 P.M.?"

- *Give more passive employees an equal opportunity to influence others and effect change.* You may have to alter how you have arrived at decisions in the past in order to draw out more passive employees. For example, if you have always created team goals in a conference room, but you have found that one employee intimidates others into agreeing with his suggestions, then do goals online this year.

Overpowering employees range from employees who let their enthusiasm run wild to employees who have some serious issues with controlling others. In either case, interventions will improve the workplace, relationships, and performance, so don't delay implementing them. The person whose relationships and productivity will improve most after this difficult process will probably be the overpowering employee him- or herself. Don't let some push-back from the employee stop you from improving his or her workplace style. After all, push-back is the overpowering employee's natural response. Once he or she realizes that you are serious about expecting change, the employee will probably apply all that energy to making the changes required.

14

The Power-Seeking Employee

Ambition can be a great motivator as long as employees continue to respect people and resources as they consider their career moves. It's when an employee gets that lean and hungry look and begins cannibalizing coworkers, relationships, and work processes to serve a solely personal agenda that a manager must step in. And wanting to move on to that next highest job is fine as long as the job an employee has his or her eye on isn't yours—a bit prematurely.

A manager must foster an atmosphere that encourages healthy ambition and a person's desire to develop into a more valuable and promotable employee. But a job is a bargain struck between an employee and a company—each must invest in the other and keep the long-term and the short-term goals of both in mind. The company should offer opportunities for advancement and developmental resources to prepare the employee for successively better positions. The employee should never consider a position to be simply a stepping-stone in his or her career. In each position, the employee should bring value to the department he or she serves and should stay long enough to make a meaningful contribution. The employee's primary focus should be on fulfilling the needs of the company in the position he or she is being paid to perform; secondarily, the employee should have an eye out for his or her own career path.

CLIMBING THE CORPORATE LADDER TOO FAST

Some employees have their priorities reversed. They are on the job only to network and to move strategically from one plum position to the next. They disregard the enriching contributions that they could make if their focus were on the job they are being paid to do. To them, performing a job well is secondary to climbing the corporate ladder. This wastes the employee's time and the company's money in the form of the costs associated with rehiring, orientation, and transition.

Blind ambition can also cost the employee more than he or she realizes. Eventually, management will recognize the employee's selfish motivations and may actually limit the employee's opportunities for a while. Teammates will also come to resent being stepped over as the power-hungry employee picks his or her way to the top. At first, excessively ambitious employees may be outwardly politically smooth, but their real motivation is to put their promotions and agendas ahead of the best interests of the team or the company. They have little regard for the welfare of others, focusing on "what's in this for me?" throughout the workday. Peers resent that when they eventually see what is going on.

The interventions in this chapter offer suggestions for dealing with these driven employees. Before you use them, however, you should allow a great deal of latitude for employees who are just eager and properly ambitious. Often these go-getters do become very successful. You may be reporting to this employee in 10 years, so don't make an unwise political move by being too harsh about the employee's high estimation of him- or herself.

Interventions

- *If you think the employee is trying to climb the corporate ladder too swiftly, present him with some case studies of people who have experienced setbacks because they moved ahead too quickly.* Stories, particularly if they are about employees in your company, are more persuasive than theories and platitudes. In most companies, vivid examples abound of employees who got in over their heads and failed or had a miserable tenure in a job. You may know of other situations in which an unseasoned employee was given a job because he had a successful mentor. When the balance of power shifted and the mentor was no longer a protector or was even fired, the poor employee found himself attacked, and his position was indefensible. Beware, however, of strenuously discouraging employees from overreaching for the gold ring. Occasionally, because of either mentors or serendipity, less experienced employees do move swiftly up the ladder. Never tell an employee that this is impossible because eventually you will be surprised by someone. The rising star should remember you as a cautious advocate, not as a critic or a career blocker.

- *Create a career path for the employee that is realistic yet intriguing to her.* Collaborate with the employee to create a realistic career path for her that shows the opportunities that she can look forward to through upward and lateral moves. In today's larger companies, most employees make many lateral moves in order to gain experience in various aspects of the business. Younger employees often have unrealistic expectations of how fast they can achieve higher positions. Companies today offer fewer upward moves than in previous decades. Management has been trimmed to create leaner organizations, and fewer positions exist. A career path should show several options and should suggest how long each step should take based on historical data. The employee should be told that no career-planning tool can predict or guarantee when or how she will be promoted. This disclaimer should be written into the plan as well.

- *Separately or in conjunction with the career path, create a development plan for the employee.* Development plans indicate professional development steps that the employee can take to increase his skills. The plan grooms the employee so that he will be ready when a good job opportunity becomes available. For example, if the employee does not know how to lead a large meeting, his development plan might require him to shadow another manager who is gifted at conducting such meetings. The employee would accompany the manager to several meetings and learn by observation. Or maybe your company requires managers to keep budget information in a database. The employee's development plan could require that he attend a class to learn to use the software that your company uses to track budget information. At least a year's worth of developmental moves should be included in the development plan. For an example, see Chapter 3.

- *Ask the employee to interview several managers or executives who achieved their positions after years of hard work.* The employee should ask these people for career advice as part of her professional development. The ambitious employee will probably enjoy the exposure to her superiors. The advice of these veterans is bound to include an admonition to "pay some dues." It's best that the employee hear these truisms from others rather than just from you.

THE EMPLOYEE WITH AN EYE ON YOUR JOB

An ambitious employee may only have one career move in mind: your job. A manager who does not realize that he or she is vulnerable to an ambitious employee's attempts to take his or her job is naive. Most people who have been in the workplace for a long time have seen this happen. Make no mistake, it is possible. Still, there are managers who experience complete disbelief when it happens to them. One reason for this is that the employee who steals a superior's job has often been an outstanding employee. In fact, this employee has probably been indispensable. The savvy manager uses appropriate interventions to retain the ambitious employee while protecting his or her own interests.

Interventions

- *If you are threatened by a subordinate who is out to usurp your job, institute a communications campaign immediately.* Communicate upward about your accomplishments more than ever before. Prepare year-end reports or a strategic business plan that highlight your present achievements and all the wonderful things you will do in the future.

    Let the ambitious employee know that you will do everything in your power to ensure that he gets your job—when you are ready to leave it.

- *Review with the employee the development plan you have created just for her.* Itemize the investments that you plan to make in her professional development, such as training, job rotations, and leadership opportunities. Offer to be her advocate in finding a promotion within another department. Ask for her support and offer yours generously.
- *Document anything that the employee has done that may be in his best interest but not the company's.* If you suspect a lack of loyalty, document the employee's developmental needs in detail during performance appraisals. The company does not need an employee moving on before his development is at the appropriate stage. If the employee is promoted too soon, he could be a danger to profits, safety, customer loyalty, and his own career.
- *Actively look for another opportunity in a different department for this employee.* No one needs to work with a power-hungry employee looking over her shoulder. Move the employee on if you are able to do it in a way that the employee will embrace. Ask your peers to look for a lateral or upward move for the employee.
- *Make sure that your name is on all work products and successes from your department.* Driven employees have a way of presenting all successes as their own and not sharing the kudos. Keep a sharp eye out for this. Put your name on cover letters, presentations, newsletter articles, and anything else that you deserve credit for managing.

Again, a little bit of ambition is a good thing. Companies are moved forward by employees who want to move forward. Encourage a healthy dose of ambition. However, if that ambition crosses the line into behaviors that undermine management, peers, or the department, take action through interventions with great haste.

15

The Unmotivated Employee

One of the most frustrating challenges a manager can face is turning around an unmotivated employee. Often these employees have the skills and intelligence to excel, but they sleepwalk through their days, investing little thought or energy in what they are doing.

Lack of motivation may be exhibited as a lack of activity in any of the following areas:

- Volunteering
- Bringing new ideas to a job
- Seeking promotion or greater responsibility
- Taking the initiative to solve problems or add value
- Participating in team or other work activities
- Discovering problems or exploring new opportunities
- Bringing energy and ideas to the workplace each day
- Investing thought, time, and self into the work at hand

These behaviors are a manager's first clues that she or he is dealing with an unmotivated employee. Naturally, the manager must determine that the employee is not impaired or unqualified for the job as covered in Chapters 4 and 19.

The next step is to have a joint goal-setting session with the employee. Once goals are set with the employee's input, as described in Chapter 2, the most critical step follows: monitoring the employee's performance and achievement of these goals. If the employee is not achieving these goals with the quality and timeliness that has been clearly agreed upon, then an intervention should be employed. People are motivated by two things: fear of punishment and hope of reward. Punishment is inherent in poor performance, since the person could lose his or her job, status, or income. It takes greater creativity to create rewards. The interventions in this chapter capitalize on the reward and punishment motivational forces. The reward interventions outnumber the punishment interventions, since a nonperforming employee has already shown a lack of responsiveness to potential punishment.

THE UNMOTIVATED PERFORMER

As established in Chapter 1, every employee would rather end the day having given a stellar performance rather than a lackluster one. That being the case, why is lack of motivation one of the most common criticisms that managers have of poorly performing employees? The reasons why employees slack off, avoid tasks, and pace themselves vary widely. Use an investigative and open-minded approach as you implement the following interventions.

Interventions

- *Ask the employee if he is concerned about performing too well and thereby having to take on greater responsibility.* Communication is the cornerstone of motivation. Some employees don't want to be promoted because they don't want the increased stress level that goes with increased responsibility. Similarly, some individual contributors don't want to be managers but prefer to continue doing the work they enjoy. Ask yourself if this is something that you can live with and that the department will perhaps benefit from. Once the employee has a chance to say that he will perform his current duties well but does not want advancement and gains your acceptance of that position, his current performance may improve greatly. Your acceptance of his continuing to do his current job at his current level may provide the safety valve that he needs in order to rid himself of destructive pressure.

- *Check first to see that you are fulfilling your responsibilities as a leader and manager.* Have you consistently conducted performance reviews to ensure that the employee realizes what your performance expectations are and what the gaps are between her performance and what is expected of her? Do you model the same work practices that you expect from others? Have you provided all the support and materials needed on a timely basis? Is your compensation in line with your competitors'? Are you hiring people who are likely to be successful, or are those you are hiring over- or underqualified? Do your part and then explore the employee's need for improvement.

- *On a similar note, demonstrate your commitment to the employee.* Employees today are often paranoid about possible downsizings. They either have experienced downsizing themselves or are surrounded by people who have been through that experience—often more than once. Tell your employee, if possible, of your intention of working through his problem of lack of motivation in order to retain him for the long term. The most unmotivating tactic is to threaten. Although there is a time and a place to be candid about consequences and even to inform the employee of potential termination, that should not be your first tactic. Affirm the employee. Praise him for the value he brings to the team. Talk about how much you want to work with him in order to motivate him to create a better work life for himself and to allow him to make even more contributions to the team.

- *For employees who do want more money or status, establish very-short-term incentives.* Unmotivated employees usually lack a long-term view. You will not win them over by telling them that they may be managing the department one day. Incentives should involve shorter time increments. Offer a one-time bonus, a dinner for two, a spare airline ticket so that a spouse can accompany the employee on a business trip, or a week of long lunch breaks to accommodate the employee's using the gym at lunch.

- *Ask the employee if she would like you to provide a personal coach or training in one area of her job.* This could be a technical skill or a tactical skill that she needs to know in order to perform better. Coaches and training can be provided from a variety of sources: outside consultants, peers, corporate training organizations, vendors, or you.

- *Determine whether there is one part of the employee's job that he dislikes so much that it is affecting his overall performance.* If that is the case, try to minimize the problem if possible. Ask other employees if anyone wants to trade for that responsibility. Some employees may not mind the task at all. If this is not practical, offer to buy a tool, software, or equipment to make the task easier. In some cases, the employee becomes overwhelmed by a certain task only once a month, or once a year if it is seasonal. Offer up to 12 days a year of temporary help to keep the employee on track. In return, ask that the employee increase his output at other times. Or reschedule the task so that the work is done weekly instead of daily, or quarterly instead of monthly.

- *Pinpoint what motivates this lackluster employee.* Motivations vary. Traditional motivators such as money, promotions, and status may not motivate this particular employee. Does quality of work life matter more to this employee? Then use funds to redesign or redecorate his workspace as an incentive. Or offer to get a cappuccino machine for the break room. Or bring in free weights and a treadmill and set up a small workout area on the floor. Or is this employee hungry for your praise and attention? Perhaps balking at work achieves the purpose of getting more interaction from you. Some people need more than a quick attaboy. For a while, do you need to be more lavish with your praise? Or is the employee very social and wants a lot of team lunches and office celebrations with cake for everyone? Offer more of this as an incentive.

- *Conduct 360°-feedback assessments for the employee.* Ask peers, subordinates, and management to give the employee feedback on her working relationships and her work habits. Honest, well-rounded feedback can sometimes be a wake-up call to unmotivated employees. There are many 360° instruments on the market, or an organizational development consultant can implement this for you.

- *Create opportunities for unmotivated employees to make greater contributions by the way you design meetings and work processes.* For example, if your team conducts project reviews monthly, create an $8\frac{1}{2} \times 11$ form that lists each project to be presented in a meeting. Require each person to write two comments about each project as they are presented, with the forms to be turned in to you. At the meeting, ask the employee to read his comments.

  Or if you manage a sales team, ask sales reps to circulate their proposals with a cover sheet to all team members. Require each team member to write a suggestion for improvement or presentation on the cover. Be sure to commend the unmotivated employee for any valuable suggestions. Once a behavior is in place, it usually lasts. If the employee develops the habit of making suggestions and receives positive reinforcement for his input, then he will probably continue to do so on a more informal basis if the cover sheet system ceases.

- *Assign the employee a mentor with whom she has a great deal in common.* Preferably, find a mentor who is only a level or two above the employee's current level. When the unmotivated employee sees someone that she likes and relates to achieving status and an improved work life, she may become motivated. The employee initially may not be able to visualize herself as an achiever. Seeing someone who is very similar to her enjoying the fruits of labor might help her to see herself as a mover and shaker also.

- *Try this exercise.* Ask the employee to tell you about the three most inspiring things he has ever experienced on the job. If he can't do this, ask him to tell you about the boss who was able to get him to achieve the most and what that boss did. Next, ask the employee to tell you the three most discouraging things he ever experienced in the work world. Empathize, but don't offer anything at first. Take this information and determine if there is a practical way to try to reward or punish him, using what you have learned.

- *Purchase motivational tapes or CDs appropriate to your industry or to the employee's job.* Ask the employee to listen to the tapes each morning as soon as she arrives. The American Management Association, Amazon.com, and many other online sources offer great motivational tapes. For some employees, this pep talk each day actually improves performance.

- *Use compelling facts and statistics to establish a clear benchmark for performance.* Some employees are subconsciously pacing themselves because they don't want to work harder than the next guy. Use anonymous statistical information to show the employee how far below the better performers he is falling. Set a benchmark and a time frame for incrementally bringing the unmotivated employee up to a level of excellent performance.

THE UNMOTIVATED TEAM MEMBER

It's one thing when the employee's performance lets the company or management down. A whole new realm of dynamics comes into play when the employee's behavior lets the team down. Before everyone's performance begins to suffer, a manager needs to take steps to increase the team member's motivation to contribute his fair share.

Interventions

- *If the employee's lack of motivation leads to negative consequences, make sure that it is the employee and not his teammates who experiences those consequences.* When one employee is not motivated, sometimes projects are delayed or processes malfunction. More motivated employees should not have to take up the slack for the unmotivated employee. Explain to the unmotivated employee that his lack of initiative may lead to the project's falling behind; therefore, the unmotivated employee, not his peers, will be required to work late. Or, if bonus money is cut and it is up to you to distribute it according to performance, warn the unmotivated employee that he will not be rewarded as much as those who bring added value and contributions to the work process. If you reward everyone, performers and nonperformers, equally, you will demoralize the strong contributors.

- *Call on the unmotivated employee more in meetings.* Or ask her ahead of time to do a brief presentation on what she is accomplishing. Sometimes, the onus of having to state one's progress on a project inspires people to create some progress—fast!
- *Ask the employee to read a book on team dynamics or business culture, such as* Who Moved My Cheese *or* The Servant. Discuss with him what he learned about himself from these books. Ask him how he thinks others may feel when he goes for more than a few weeks without volunteering or making helpful suggestions.
- *Employees who are not motivated by you may be highly motivated by peer recognition.* Here are some ideas that are working in some companies, as described by Gregory P. Smith in *Tips and Techniques: Dynamic Ways to Reward, Energize & Motivate Your Team.*

  - "Employee Dollars. At Phoenix Solutions Inc. employees award an 'employee dollar' to fellow employees who do something special or exceed company expectations. Each month the employee with the most 'dollars' gets movie tickets, dinner, and a plaque with their name as 'Employee of the Month.'
  - "Man Overboard Award. CIGNA believes in rewarding employees who go over and beyond for their customers. The Man Overboard Award is a life-saving ring, which the president presents to an employee at a special ceremony. CIGNA also pays teams for implemented ideas that improve productivity with awards as high as $25,000.
  - "Engineering Bucks. The technicians at Weather Channel in Atlanta created their own recognition system—called Tech Bucks. All they did was Xerox a dollar bill and give five of them out at the beginning of each month. They give them to each other for doing a good job. At the end of the month they tally up who got the most and the winner gets a special prize.
  - "Dancing the Macarena. Employees at PeopleSoft, Inc. still haven't forgotten the day that CEO David Duffield danced the Macarena in front of 500 happy co-workers. Duffield does not act like a boss. His office is a cubicle; he answers his own phone and opens his own mail. Annual employee turnover is three percent, or one-quarter of the national average. Employees who earn outstanding service awards get either $500 in cash or 100 stock options.
  - "Thrilling Thursdays. Nike Employees in Beaverton, Oregon can't wait for Thursday to roll around. They stop work at 4:30 in the afternoon . . . they kayak across a lake, race bikes and compete in a 600-yard run."

- *Create a peer award that is given monthly to the strongest contributor on the team.* Make sure it carries with it a gift certificate or a free dinner for two. Have peers vote on the person who contributes the most in terms of time, ideas, initiative, and energy.
- *Hire an expert to do team-building exercises with your staff.* Be sure the exercises address the work process, workload, or workflow. It is key that employees who contribute little realize the impact that this behavior has on the team.

The most important point in dealing with sluggish employees is to do something sooner rather than later. Everyone has days or weeks of diminished motivation. Responding to signs of poor motivation and addressing it are the most productive things a manager can do in order to prevent poor motivation from becoming an ongoing problem. Chapter 10, "The Unproductive Employee," also offers many interventions to help unmotivated employees turn their performance around.

16

The Employee Who Complains or Gossips

Some employees are always just a little bit unhappy about something. They complain if they are not chosen for plum assignments, but when they are chosen for those assignments, they complain that they always have to do the big jobs. Or, their physical environment is too hot, too cold, too drab, too colorful, too remotely located, too accessible, too busy, too uncomfortable, too outdated, or too poorly designed. They hated the last manager, but the new one is even worse. They are repositories of negative information and gossip about everyone, and they take malicious joy in spreading that information. And don't think that because you are their confidante, you are immune; eventually, they will share something negative about you.

When an employee invests so much energy in such heightened sensitivity and complaint, that employee robs the department of his or her best effort to accomplish the work. An even greater problem is the way this negativity spreads to everyone around the employee. Even excellent employees can be temporarily distracted or even discouraged by negative talk. In so many ways, productivity and morale are damaged by habitual complaining and negative talk.

All leaders should welcome a certain amount of dissent or complaint—don't get me wrong. Great managers make employees feel free to bring legitimate complaints up for discussion. The employees addressed in this chapter abuse that privilege. They find reasons to offer frequent criticism of the department, the company, their coworkers, and others. The criticism they offer far outweighs the praise, support, and attaboys that should be the hallmarks of a healthy team.

THE EMPLOYEE WHO COMPLAINS ABOUT THE WORKPLACE

Employees who complain about everything from corporate policies to the new paint color on the walls are rarely satisfied no matter what you do. In some cases, all you can do is reduce the number of complaints they make and work with them to improve their attitudes a bit each year. The interventions in this chapter are ways to address the deluge of complaints that these negative individuals present.

Interventions

- *Whenever possible, appoint your chronic complainers to focus groups or committees that create policies and changes.* Complaints are reduced when the employee is part of the group that is responsible for the policies and decisions. Also, you are making use of the complainer's critical eye. It is actually an asset to have these folks express their concerns over issues before anything new is rolled out across the board. They may voice criticism that others who don't speak up feel the same way about. Not all the criticism that a complainer offers is invalid; you need to learn how to capitalize on the useful information that you receive from complainers.

- *Arrive at consensus with your team about environmental issues: thermostat settings, design or decorating decisions that are within your control, playing or not playing music, or anything else that touches the work space of the complaining employee.* Conduct a yearly survey on issues that have been points of complaint in the past. Tell each employee that you are going to make decisions democratically, by allowing the group to vote on what makes them most comfortable. Warn them, however, that after the survey there can be no complaints or conversations about the decision for 1 year. If an employee is dissatisfied with the environment in some way, tell him that you must take into account the needs of the entire team and that the team has spoken. Tell him that you cannot give him preferential treatment.

- *If your workplace environment is dictated by a building engineer or is otherwise beyond your control, offer to conduct a workplace complaint meeting with the employee.* Prepare a workplace complaint form ahead of time. The form need not be complex; just put "workplace complaint" at the top in all caps and bold and put a place for the employee to sign his name. The rest of the form can be a large box in the center in which the employee can write her complaint(s).

The primary purpose of the meeting is to brainstorm ways to remedy the situation that is bothering the employee. You may ask what the employee can do to solve the problem and what she wants to have happen. Occasionally, just asking the employee these questions squelches the complaints because some people really don't want anything specific—they just enjoy complaining. If the employee comes up with a workable solution, then try to support her in implementing it.

The secondary reason for using the workplace complaint meeting and form is to discourage chronic complainers. There is something about having to make an official complaint and sign one's name to it that gives most employees pause. Few employees want to have a whole drawerfull of complaints documenting their negativity in the boss's possession. The employee may blithely fill out the form and complain the first time, but as she considers documenting her dissatisfaction time after time, she will probably stop and reconsider at least a few of her complaints.

Be sure to implement this across the department and not with just one or two employees. Again, you must be careful to maintain an open-door policy that encourages employees to come to you with legitimate and even helpful complaints. You might even announce the new system in language that urges people to still come to you but conveys that you are trying to stem the tide of frivolous complaints. Most employees will know exactly for whom the system was designed. They may be as tired of hearing the complaints as you are.

- *Get an expert involved if you are in a medium to large company.* For example, if the temperature seems too hot or cold for the employee, set up an appointment with the maintenance supervisor or the building engineer for the employee. And if the employee complains about the newest benefits package, offer to set up an appointment with HR for the employee to find out why this package was chosen. Begin to offer information in a way that does not depend on the employee's constantly bending your ear and everyone else's. Often, the employee is simply seeking attention and an audience. People can always find someone to listen to negative comments. Going straight into problem-solving mode is very dissatisfying to a complainer. You want to avoid rewarding unproductive behavior, and passing the employee on to an informed person outside the department is highly unrewarding.

- *Counsel the employee and give him a more balanced view based on facts and statistics.* For one quarter, monitor all the complaints that you receive from all employees. In a sit-down meeting with the complainer, give him the straight facts. For example, you might say, "Our workgroup has 14 people. In the last 12 weeks, I have received a total of six complaints; half of them have come from one person, you. We all have things that we have to compromise on or that we wish were better. I am asking you to consider the possibility that your expectations about how comfortable the workplace can be might be unrealistic. Will you think about that? Let's meet again exactly 1 week from today at this same time and place to discuss what you think. I am open to considering anything you have to say, but I am trying to reduce the negative talk out on the floor, since it can hurt the productivity of the other team members."

　　Even if the employee defensively justifies his complaints and asserts that his expectations are very realistic, the message you are sending will discourage him from coming to you with the next frivolous complaint. He will remember this conversation and ask himself how realistic the complaint is before he casually starts complaining. If he doesn't put this type of thought into it, you may have an employee with very poor judgment who may be hurting you in other areas as well.

EMPLOYEES WHO GOSSIP OR COMPLAIN ABOUT COWORKERS

Criticizing or gossiping about coworkers may be the greatest blow to productivity in the office environment. Gossip is costly, not to mention painful, whether the target is a peer, the boss, or a subordinate. This behavior is the antithesis of teamwork, which companies invest so much money in developing. Here are just a few of the losses that companies experience when employees disparage their coworkers.

- Time spent gossiping or complaining
- Time that management spends dealing with the resulting problems
- Lack of cooperation and synergy among team members
- Slowing of the work process as a result of ineffective communication
- Potential problem-solving or even disciplinary meetings
- Possible loss of a valuable employee and the associated costs of recruitment and training
- Work slowdown resulting from suffering or anxiety over hurtful remarks

The list could continue, but you get the drift. A wise person once said that the greatest theft is stealing from a person's reputation. Some employees who would never steal a paper clip regularly gossip and steal from coworkers' reputations. The following interventions deal with this counterproductive behavior.

Interventions

- *Have a frank discussion with the employee about gossiping.* Most gossipers don't view themselves as gossipers. They are often surprised to find out that their behind-the-back comments are common knowledge. For some, having their behavior acknowledged is all it takes to end their habit of disparaging others. Ask for the employee's help in doing some team building. Say something to the effect that the whole team is affected when one team member says uncomplimentary things about another team member. Tell the employee that you would appreciate it if she would work toward sharing only information that will encourage and build up other members of the team. Ask her to actively look for opportunities to say positive things about others.

- *Give the employee some guidelines to follow when he has information about others that is not complimentary.* Because people do have to share uncomplimentary information at times, give the employee your guidelines for sharing such information. You may want to include some of the following:
  - The gossiping employee should first go to the person being talked about to determine if the information is true and to find ways to work through any problems at that level.
  - If there is no productive reason to share information, then don't share it.
  - Negative information about others should be shared on a need-to-know basis. If the gossiping employee starts to share some juicy information, he should first ask himself, "Does the person I am telling this to actually need to know it?" If the answer is no, the employee should not tell it.
  - Before sharing negative information in the future, ask the employee to run it by you first.
- *Educate the employee about gossip.* Tell her that much of it is untrue and most of it is harmful in some way. Inform her that even true gossip reflects more negatively on the teller than on the victim. Gossip is a form of theft, stealing something that is more valuable than money. And untrue gossip can even cost the employee a fortune in legal fees and damages if someone decides to prosecute for slander.
- *Ask the employee to avoid people or places that encourage gossip for a while.* Some areas, like smoking areas and break rooms, are known for inciting gossip. If an employee can avoid the areas

where he is most tempted to gossip, he will be more successful in breaking this habit.

- *Hold a team meeting and initiate an antigossip campaign.* Encourage employees to "just say no" to gossip. Require employees to say two positive things every time they must say one negative thing about another employee's performance. For example, "David did not get the article to me in time to get it into this month's newsletter, but the graphics he created will make twice the impact when we get it into next month's edition. He had a great idea for sending the idea out via email in the meantime."
- *Ask the employee if she is unhappy in some area.* Employees who tear down others are often insecure or unhappy in some professional or personal area. Try to build the employee up or offer counseling. You might consider asking her if she finds the person she is gossiping about to be a threat to her in any area of work.
- *Ask the employee to go to the person he is gossiping about and try to build a relationship with her.* It is more difficult to gossip about someone whom you know and like.

Complaining employees often develop many of the problems discussed in other chapters, such as the chapters on employees who are unmotivated, angry, or laden with personal problems. In particular, see the discussion of the chatty employee in Chapter 8 for additional interventions.

17

The Employee Who Mismanages Priorities or Experiences Burnout

Some employees can't handle everything that is on their plates because they mismanage their priorities. Other employees become overloaded because too much has been delegated to them by management or given to them by default when coworkers are less industrious. In either case, finding out who is at fault is not the issue. Solving the problem before a good employee experiences burnout is what's important to both the employee and the company.

THE OVERWORKED EMPLOYEE

It always amazes me when managers try to increase an employee's productivity by throwing more work at him or her. Management's first concern should be the employee's ability to successfully master today's workload.

In some cases, the employee is legitimately overworked. Managers often think that because the manager herself completed a certain list of tasks when she was in the employee's position, the employee should be able to do the same. Before you write off a great employee as a laggard, consider these points:

- Some jobs are more complex today than they were a few years ago. Bank tellers today perform tasks that stockbrokers and loan officers once did. Tellers don't simply execute transactions today. They sell—and their list of products is long and sophisticated.
- Reception jobs have changed since 9/11. Screening for security purposes may take twice as long.

What about the positions you manage? What has changed since you held those positions? Are you factoring those changes into your calculations of each employee's workload? Are the employees perhaps working harder because their responsibilities have expanded?

Like the great employees mentioned in Chapter 5, overworked employees can lose their incentive and decrease their productivity. See that chapter for strategies that will help you retain employees who have perhaps worked too much and not too little.

EMPLOYEES WHO MISMANAGE WORK PRIORITIES

Arriving at work, an employee today is whacked with multiple tasks, almost all of them marked *Urgent*. Multiple priorities battle to get ahead of another on the employee's to-do list. The boss may think task 14 on your to-do list should be number 1. Internal or external customers are bringing pressure to bear on tasks 3 through 7. The employee may see that task 8 needs to be moved to the top of the list in order to avoid creating a bottleneck for a peer department. What do some employees do in the face of screaming multiple priorities? They shut down or slow down. Maybe this is not intentional, but many employees see the impossibility of pleasing everyone and begin to sleepwalk through their jobs.

Interventions

- *To the degree possible, codify your priorities.* If irate customers should always go to the head of the priority list, put that in a written policy. Share the policy with peer departments and other management. Having such a written policy allows the employee to embark on a path of action quickly and thus improve his productivity. Without a policy stating which tasks to tackle first, second, and third, the swamped employee may spend a huge part of the workday evaluating priorities and justifying his position to stakeholders. The written policy allows him to take the Nike approach and "Just do it." It also runs interference and keeps the employee from being the bad guy when he has to serve a customer ahead of a coworker.

- *When you assign projects, give the employee your view—explicitly—of the status or priority of that project.* If the project is a low priority, say something like, "We won't need this until June, so your Product Launch Event takes priority over this. Just be ready by June 1."
- *Enroll the employee in a time management class or a class on managing multiple priorities.* The employee may just need some training on organizing time, delegating, and scheduling efficiently.
- *Consider assertiveness training if the employee just can't say no.* Some employees take on more work than they can handle by volunteering too much to help others, cover phones, or work on committees. There are times when it is appropriate to say no. If you suspect that the employee needs to stand up and set some boundaries with peers or even customers, enroll her in an assertiveness class for professionals. After the class, work with the employee to identify times when it's appropriate for her to say to the coworker in her doorway, "This is not a good time."
- *Go back to the will do/won't do grid in Chapter 4 and determine the source of the mismanagement problem.* The interventions just given largely apply to employees who can't manage their time and workload. What if the problem is that the employee is unwilling to prioritize in the way you believe is most productive?

First, explain to the employee that your view of what needs to be done is based on the needs of the greater organization. Explain some of those needs that the employee may not be considering. Second, ask if there is anything that you personally have done that is causing or contributing to the problem and how you might remedy that. Third, be prepared to offer an incentive or a consequence if the problem is not solved. This third step should take place only after a couple of friendly conversations regarding the employee's lack of cooperation. Give the employee ample time to turn his behavior around before enforcing consequences like a reprimand, removal from a project, a lowered performance rating, or documentation in his file.

EMPLOYEES SUFFERING FROM BURNOUT

Burnout is an epidemic that is affecting our best workers. No company, no matter how great, can completely prevent some hard-working employees from experiencing burnout. Often the best employees will take on too much in an effort to please their superiors or because they have fears related to job security. Their insecurities may be holdovers from childhood and have nothing to do with the workload. Even a great employee who is driven to the point where her or his life is out of balance will demonstrate signs of burnout, such as the following:

- Fatigue, listlessness
- Lower productivity
- Lack of enthusiasm and initiative
- More frequent absences or tardiness
- Failure to grasp concepts as quickly
- Impatience or irritability
- Complaining

The following interventions offer suggestions for combating these symptoms.

Interventions

- *Encourage the employee to achieve greater balance in his life.* Some companies even pay for health club or golf club memberships for valuable employees. They know that these fringe benefits will strengthen the employee in many ways. Sometimes you must verbalize your support for the employee's walking away from work at the end of the day to spend time with his family, on church activities, or on hobbies. Talk to the employee about the balance in his life, and show your support.

- *Temporarily relieve the employee of some tasks or assign the employee a temp to rid her of that feeling of being overwhelmed with tasks.* Stress that this change is temporary until the two of you can find a long-term solution. Then communicate regularly with the employee to find solutions.
- *Give the employee a break or a job rotation.* Give the employee a long weekend to rest and rejuvenate. Try to show support for the employee's efforts to recharge his batteries. In some cases, an employee simply can't see a way to change his priorities, trim his work, or take control of his schedule. In that case, a job rotation might be in order. As a developmental move, ask the employee to do an entirely different job for a while. Or ask him to work in a totally different part of the company. The employee may be more successful in designing a new job than in getting his old one under control. When he returns to his old job more refreshed, he may be better able to set boundaries.
- *For long-term employees, sabbaticals or offsite educational programs may provide the break they need to bring their life back into balance.* Executive MBA programs abound today. Study programs such as these provide a few weeks away from the job and give the added benefit of allowing the employee to learn ideas from other companies that can enhance her or his department. Consider sponsoring an employee for some offsite training, preferably a boarding or residential program so that the employee can totally get away.
- *Give the employee a slightly longer lunch hour for a while so that she can exercise or take a walk.* If it works best for the employee, give this extra time at the end or beginning of the day.
- *Offer the employee time with a counselor or therapist.* Sometimes repressed anger or frustration leads to burnout. Your company psychologist or a therapist may be helpful if the employee voluntarily wishes to have this type of help.
- *Encourage the employee to have a physical.* Thyroid or hormonal problems or low-grade infections can cause people to be unable to cope with a workload that they once handled easily.

In short, many factors can lead to burnout. Everyone seems to be working harder today, so truly overworked employees are harder to identify. If an employee you manage demonstrates the symptoms of burnout, invest in interventions immediately. Employees who are experiencing burnout can be rehabilitated and become top performers on your team.

18

The Angry Employee

Anger impedes problem solving, blocks work processes from functioning efficiently, and harms productivity in myriad ways. In other words, people don't think as well, work as well, or cooperate as well when they are angry. The bigger problem is that the people around the angry people suffer the same symptoms.

Doctors have long known the destructive effects of anger on our hearts, our digestive tracts, and our immune systems. The stress associated with it has been linked to everything from the common cold to cancer. Anger in the workplace wields its destructive power in similar ways. Usually, anger works silently and insidiously. Occasionally, it can erupt into violence.

Responsible managers deal with the angry employee sooner rather than later. Less serious problems with anger can usually be resolved fairly quickly if they are addressed early enough. If a manager refuses to acknowledge an employee's anger or underestimates the degree of that anger, outbursts or even violence can occur. The interventions in this chapter give suggestions for dealing with four types of angry employees: those with generalized anger, those who are angry with a manager, those who are angry with a coworker, and those for whom anger has the potential for violence. Read all four sections, since the interventions for one category often work well for another.

THE EMPLOYEE WITH GENERALIZED ANGER

This employee seethes or pouts or scowls. He may make unnecessarily loud noises, such as stomping his feet as he walks or slamming desk drawers. On the other hand, he may keep his anger bottled up and wear a pained and martyred expression as he silently sleepwalks through his angry day. Angry people express their anger in hundreds of diverse ways. Here are just a few of the ways in which some very different angry folks have communicated their anger to their coworkers:

- Sharp or malicious remarks
- Grabbing things or other abrupt gestures
- A raised voice
- Refusal to cooperate—openly or passively
- Clipped syllables
- Extreme criticism or attacks on coworkers
- Sarcasm
- Criticizing by joking when others are serious
- Setting others up to fail
- Uncalled-for or extreme complaining

There may be no one particular thing that sets this employee off; instead, every little thing seems to incense her anew. Like the complaining employee in Chapter 16 (recommended reading), the angry employee may be impossible to placate because the problem may be deep-rooted. The employee's anger may be a companion that the employee has carried around since childhood and may be about old issues unrelated to the workplace. You cannot resolve family and personal issues that this employee may be in denial about. You can only hope that the interventions in this section will resolve the problems on the job that are preventing the employee from fully achieving success.

Interventions

- *Meeting one: In a sit-down meeting devoted totally to improving the employee's work life, ask him what you as his manager can do to improve conditions for him.* Do not combine this meeting with a performance appraisal or other objectives. When you set up the meeting, tell the employee that this meeting is focused solely on making conditions better for him. At the beginning of the meeting, state your commitment to improving conditions. Acknowledge that you see signs that the employee is unhappy and that you want to do your part to remedy that. You may want to consider not discussing consequences with the employee in this first meeting. If the employee's anger has caused serious problems, however, you will need to bring that up at this time. The outcome of the meeting will be one of these possibilities:

- The employee will tell you something that is a valid reason for his being angry, you will fix it, and the problem will blow over. Often employees are excellent at brainstorming their own solutions.
- The employee will vent his anger over trivial things, appreciate the attention you are giving him, and stop taking out his anger in the workplace, and the problem will blow over.
- The employee will continue to be angry and will reject solutions or comfort, and the problem will remain.
- The employee will grow angrier for irrational reasons as he begins to talk, and the problem will remain.
- The meeting will communicate to the employee that his behavior has attracted serious attention, and he will take steps to control his anger on his own out of fear or maturity.
- The meeting will communicate to the employee that his behavior has attracted serious attention, and he will repress his anger for a while, but it will reemerge in another form later.

The main objective of this first meeting is for you to spend a great deal of time listening to the employee. The employee should do most of the talking, so use plenty of open questions and sympathetic nods. The meeting format goes something like this:

- State your sincere interest in the employee's happiness and success in his present position.
- State that it concerns you when one of your employees seems unhappy. *Anger* is too threatening a word for most employees.

- Ask what you can do to improve conditions.
- As the employee talks, use open questions or statements to encourage him to open up: "Tell me about that," "Describe some situations," "How does that compare to other places you have worked?" "What would be an ideal way to handle that?"
- Close by first telling the employee what you *can* do. If he has mentioned even one item that you can change for him, start with that and agree to do it. Second, assure him that you will be considering other improvements if possible. Third, ask if he thinks that the changes you have agreed to will help to make him more satisfied at work. If he says yes, you may not need a second meeting. Instead, suggest that the employee be the one to schedule a second meeting. Say, "I scheduled this meeting because I wanted to help you feel better about coming to work. I am going to leave the second meeting up to you. If you feel your dissatisfaction growing, please communicate with me by asking for a second meeting."
- *Meeting two: Meeting two is not punitive, but the employee should be charged with the responsibility for changing.* At this point, the employee should be informed that angry, nonproductive behavior in the workplace may have consequences. The format of this meeting should be the following:
  - Thank the employee for investing time in resolving this problem. State that you are optimistic that with both of you investing time in problem solving, the situation should improve.
  - Ask the employee if he thinks that his unhappiness affects anyone or anything at work besides him. Allow him to talk about that by asking open questions.
  - Tell him that you feel that his anger has affected the workplace. Ask him if any of the concessions or changes from the first meeting are improving the situation.
  - Tell him that you are hoping for even greater improvement and that you are willing to invest in that. Offer one or more of the following to help the employee:
    - Counseling by a local or internal psychologist

- Time to go to a weekly appointment with a counselor of his choice
- Meeting with you weekly for a month to work through workplace issues
- An extra day off with pay to create a long weekend to think things over and resolve some things in his own mind
- An offer of your own design that fits this unique situation
- State that you value him greatly, but that you are responsible for making everything run smoothly for a dozen other employees, so you must ask that he make dealing with his anger a priority. At this point, you may want to inform him of possible consequences if he continues his angry behavior. The employee should be informed and given ample time to change before consequences are imposed.
- Again, tell him that you are supporting him in his efforts to resolve his anger and encourage him to come to you if he needs further help. End on a positive note.
- Agree to meet again, and set a definite time and place.
- *Meeting three: If all goes well, meeting three will be a meeting to congratulate the employee on making great progress in resolving his anger issues.* If that is the case, point out improvements that you have noticed, ask if you can help further, and set a time to check back in on this in 30 to 90 days.
  - If the employee's anger problem has not improved, it is time to consider a more drastic step. Before you do that, consider what the employee's response might be. If this is an employee you cannot afford to lose, consider repeating meeting two instead of proceeding. Also, if this is an employee who makes you uncomfortable or who has the potential to be volatile, do not conduct this meeting by yourself. An experienced human resources professional would be a great choice to advise you or accompany you on the next step. Depending on the employee, the company, the situation, and many other factors, you might choose one of the following steps:
    - Require the employee to seek intensive counseling.

- Have the employee participate in an Employee Assistance Program (described in Chapter 19).
- Ask the employee to apologize to his coworkers and accept the consequences for problems that his anger may have caused.
- Ask the employee to keep a journal of everything that angers or annoys him for 2 weeks. At the end of those 2 weeks, discuss those items that the employee is willing to share. Ask the employee to mark all items either "+" for "in my control," "?" for "somewhat in my control," or "–" for "out of my control." Remind him that one thing that can make an item be in his control is to bring the problem to you. (Of course, you don't want to say that if this is an employee who already abuses your time.)
- Explore whether there are health factors that are creating or exacerbating the anger. Suggest exercise, more rest, a physical, and a look at nutrition. Some employees snap when they have had too much caffeine or their muscles are taut from stress or they lack oxygen as a result of artery problems or lack of exercise. Encourage the employee to attack this problem physically.
- Encourage the employee to volunteer at charities where great need or serious illness is a way of life. You can't force an employee to work for a charity, but you can suggest that the volunteer work might help his spirits. One of the greatest cures for anger is to see others who have real needs and have some monumental things that they could be mad at the world about. Doing things for others decreases one's focus on oneself and the imperfections of one's own life. Also, the positive examples set by some truly abused or needy people can be inspiring. The employee's problems may pale in comparison.
- Require that the employee attend anger management or conflict resolution classes. Personal coaches also do this type of training.
- If the anger is passive-aggressive, consider holding team-building activities to draw out the hidden anger. Tell the facilitator your objective beforehand.

THE EMPLOYEE WHO IS ANGRY WITH THE MANAGER

Showing the boss that you are angry with her carries risks. That's why you may not know that an employee is seething with anger at the sight of you. Not all employees will be foolhardy enough to confront you directly or display angry outbursts or show typical anger symptoms. Some will give you the silent treatment. Take note if an employee is eerily quiet. If looks could kill, many bosses would be dead today from the nonverbal signals from angry employees. Other employees will be balky and uncooperative. A few manipulative ones will get other people to tell you what they want conveyed. If the object of the employee's anger is you, he will usually change his behavior toward you in some way. Use the same interventions used with generalized anger, but modify the script and consider adding the following suggestions.

Interventions

- *Earnestly explore your role in provoking the anger by self-examination, querying the staff, and weighing the employee's allegations.* Remedy what you can.
- *Write a letter from the employee's point of view.* This role-playing exercise is designed to put you in the employee's position and increase your empathy for her issues. Pretend that you are the employee and that you are writing a letter to your best friend. In the letter, you (as the angry employee) are telling your best friend about all the injustices that have been done to you. As you write in this other persona, your ability to see the situation from the employee's point of view should increase.
- *Ask a human resources consultant or representative to conduct conflict resolution exercises with the employee and you.* These professionals are skilled in creating win-win situations by objectively working through problems.
- *If the employee is angry because he was passed over for a promotion or a raise, create a plan jointly that will lead to a similar promotion or raise in the future.* Focus on the future and don't try to force the employee to agree with you about the past decision.

Tell the employee, "I realize that I gave John the promotion instead of you and that you had seniority. John landed the position because he had the skills to handle the budget. I want to plan a path for you to your next promotion so that you will never lose a promotion for that reason again. The first thing I want you to do is to start taking some of the responsibility for helping me with the budget each month. Second, I am sending you to the class "Accounting for Managers," which will be held on June 25. I hope that we can work together more amiably than we have been lately. You might not agree with my decision, but going forward I will help you in any way I can."

- *If the problem is personality style differences, ask an industrial psychologist to administer the Myers-Briggs or some other style difference instrument.* Then work with the psychologist on some exercises that will increase the employee's and your appreciation of various personality styles. The psychologist can also show you how to adapt your styles successfully to each other.

- *Compile three lists: things the employee and I agree on, things we will never agree on, and things we can discuss and perhaps compromise on.* Ask the employee to compile the same three lists. Sit together and compare the lists. Agree to work on the areas of potential compromise. This exercise begins to encourage the employee to drop futile feuds and complaints.

- *Avoid "clipping" while listening.* Clipping is the habit of jumping in too fast as soon as someone has finished his or her last syllable. The term comes from the fact that if the listener jumps in with a comment too swiftly, he or she may actually clip off the last syllable of the other person's last word. Be sure to make the employee feel thoroughly listened to. Pause at the end of the employee's comments for at least 2 seconds—just in case she is not finished. Make her feel that you sincerely want to hear her views. Also, be sure to have a pleasant and interested facial expression. Nonverbal communication is powerful at moments like this.

- *Be particularly sensitive and practice empathy skills in the following situations: performance appraisals, giving constructive feedback or criticism, changing any element of the employee's job, and other such touchy situations.* Few people are truly comfortable with being evaluated or with change. These situations are rife with opportunities for anger. Proceed cautiously and plan ahead what you will say.

THE EMPLOYEE WHO IS ANGRY WITH A COWORKER

One angry employee can poison a department and make morale dismal. What a waste of time—both the angry employee's time and that of coworkers who have to listen to him or her. Angry employees can cause rifts between others in the department who originally worked well together. Feuds in some departments have lasted for years. And the fuming employees don't just tell their woes one time and have done with it; they tell people over and over again.

Modifications of all the interventions in this chapter can be used when an employee is angry with another employee. In addition, the following interventions will help you avoid the creation of a toxic workplace.

Interventions

- *Conduct team-building exercises or hire a professional trainer or consultant to do team-building exercises with you.* Whether you try to do the exercises just for the two affected employees or for the entire team, these exercises can bring about greater cooperation and draw out differences and address them.
- *Counsel each employee separately.* Ask each employee for his or her grievances and attempt to garner compromise and concessions from each. If that doesn't work, counsel both of them together. Avoid taking sides, and don't allow the angry employee to talk derogatorily about the other employee.
- *Try this empathy-building exercise in a meeting with both employees.* Tell the angry employee that for 5 minutes she must listen to the other employee talk about how it feels to be the object of so much anger. The angry employee cannot interrupt or contradict— even if she feels that the whole conversation is bogus. Then require the angry employee to make three empathy statements that

show compassion for the other employee—even if she does not agree with what was said. Examples of empathy statements can be found in Chapter 3.

After the other employee tells his side of the story, it is the angry employee's turn to vent, and her partner must make three empathy statements to her. After this first round, each employee gets an additional 2 minutes to vent, and the listener must make one more empathy statement. Then the discussion is cut off. The two coworkers depart to separate rooms to write down all rebuttal, defensive remarks, corrections of facts, and other comments. A copy of this is given to the other employee and to the manager.

Then the manager does a version of the three lists exercise mentioned earlier. The manager creates a list of the things both employees agree on, a list of things they must agree to disagree on and leave alone, and a list of things that they will work on together to make compromises and concessions. The manager presents the lists to both employees and opens a discussion with them in a joint meeting. A variation of this is to have each employee do this separately and then merge the lists.

- *There may come a time when all these interventions have been tried and the manager needs to go to the employee and counsel him to let go of his anger over a futile issue.* Some employees are irrationally angry with other employees as a result of jealousy or prejudice or something that is out of the manager's control. After making an effort to be reasonable and compassionate, the manager should go to the angry employee and advise him to let the issue drop and to mend the relationship, or else there will be damage to the department and perhaps to the employee's reputation and performance.

- *Pair the two employees up or separate them completely.* Anger can sometimes be dissipated in two opposite ways: working together closely or spending time completely apart. As a manager, you will have to decide which method to try first. In some cases, an angry employee just needs time to cool off and get her perspective back. Putting the two employees in separate places or assigning them to disparate projects is a great way for some feuds to die a natural death.

In other cases, the employees will benefit from being thrown together for a while. Working closely together to achieve a common goal can sometimes make friends out of almost enemies. This sounds like a strange approach, but it is occasionally effective. The angry employee may begin to see other dimensions of her coworker and to understand him and his motivations better.

WHEN ANGER HAS THE POTENTIAL FOR VIOLENCE

One out of five workers has been angry enough to hurt another employee within the last 5 years, according to a recent Gallup poll. That's a lot of anger. The solutions in this chapter have been aimed at airing differences and fostering solutions. Some employees repress their anger and may not even show outward signs of being very angry people. These are the most dangerous types. Holding back valid or invalid anger for long periods of time can lead to outbursts or even violence.

According to the National Institute for Occupational Safety and Health, over a thousand workplace homicides occur each year, in addition to more than a million assaults. Over half of these occur in the service or retail sectors, and the numbers have been steadily increasing since the 1990s. Being watchful for employees who may be simmering volcanoes of anger is just good business sense.

How can you spot an employee who may become violent? Although there is no exact profile, one characteristic that is predominant is that such employees are usually loners. Often they are not considered particularly hostile people, but coworkers tend to say that violent employees previously kept to themselves. It is for this reason and many more that team integration and collaboration are so important.

In addition to the interventions already mentioned, try the following.

Interventions

- *Don't go it alone.* Ask for advice, help, and support from your superiors and peers. Identifying someone as potentially dangerous is difficult and may leave you legally vulnerable. For that reason, include your boss, the owner (if this is a small business), mental health professionals, and any other resources who can aid you in making this call. The object is to help the angry employee—not to damage his reputation. Guarding the employee's privacy and dignity are top priority. Consider consulting your company's attorney about what you can do and say regarding this sensitive employee.

- *Work to integrate the employee socially into the team.* Place the employee on committees where you think she will be successful, take the employee and another employee with whom she has much in common out to lunch, sponsor the employee for organizations within the company such as service organizations, and work to draw her into conversations on the floor.

- *If your company's attorney or human resources professional agrees that you can proceed, insist that the employee get counseling.* Often these employees are depressed and will not seek help unless they are required to do so.

- *Never meet with the employee alone or go offsite with her by yourself.* Use caution in your dealings with this potentially volatile person.

Whether the employee is temporarily angry over a valid issue or is seriously angry and potentially violent, the manager has an obligation to initiate communication and aid in solving the problem. Managers who are averse to conflict may not confront workplace anger. Doing nothing exacerbates the behavior and can lead to even more people suffering consequences. Timely implementation of interventions can diminish an employee's anger and restore harmony to a team.

19

The Employee with Personal Problems or Addictions

Everyone has personal problems. Some people bring more than their share of these problems into the workplace. Although sympathy should be shown when an employee has a run of one personal problem after another, experienced managers know that some employees capitalize on life's misfortunes to come in late, take excessive days off for appointments, or handle personal business by phone. Even if the employee is on the job, she may impair her own productivity and that of everyone else as she bemoans one sad circumstance in her life after another. Addictive behaviors, such as a serious drug problem, can be even more distracting and destructive to work processes.

More difficult to handle are employees who do not share their problems or addictions on the job, but whose work begins to suffer and whose behavior deteriorates as a cry for help. Managers must walk a fine line between being interested in a sensitive way and respecting an employee's right to privacy. The following interventions are helpful in dealing with troubled employees before their problems result in serious difficulties for the department, coworkers, and management. You should discuss these interventions with your company's attorney before implementing them to ensure that you are not vulnerable to legal action. Often employees with personal problems are looking for someone to blame and may develop a victim mentality. Protect yourself by investing in expert advice from a labor attorney who can guide you through the individual situation.

FIRST STEPS IN MANAGING THE ADDICTIVE OR TROUBLED PERSONALITY

Consider the employee's history. Is this a long-time employee who previously has been a consistent performer? Allowing employees who have had great attendance and a good work ethic some time to work things out makes good business sense. The employee will probably return to his or her usual standard of performance after this season of difficulty. It will take you an equal amount of time to hire and train a replacement, and the new employee may not be as satisfactory.

New employees are a different story. Some employees have a history of starting jobs with great enthusiasm, but as their enthusiasm wanes, they suddenly have a plethora of sick relatives to deal with or ailments of their own. Or an old addiction may recur. This spotty job history may not have been reflected on the employee's résumé, and former employers are not forthcoming about voicing their suspicions for fear of being sued.

Interventions

- *You must have a written policy in place for dealing with absences due to personal problems as well as those due to illness.* Invest in the aid of a labor attorney or the Small Business Association to help you create a solid one. The policy should state clearly your methods and procedures for dealing with excessive personal problems, drugs in the workplace, and addictive behaviors. If you do not have an established policy in place before you need it, your company is limited in what it can do with an affected employee.
- *Before you hire someone, ask the employee to read and sign your policies, including the ones that relate to drugs, excessive sick days, performance, and other related problems.* Require every current employee to read the policies and sign the forms. Keep these signed forms on file, just in case.

- *Never accuse an employee of addiction or a similar problem, and train your supervisors to handle personal problems with sensitivity and professionalism.* Supervisors and employers can discuss only performance issues with the employees. These discussions must be highly objective and must not reflect judgment, suspicion, or gossip. In other words, you can say, "Your number of sick days exceeds your annual allotment of 13 days," or "You are handling only 30 customer service calls a day and the department average is 40." These are objective indicators of poor performance; as an employer, you may address these. You may not make comments such as, "You seem to be in a bad mood lately" or "You're not having problems with your teenager again, are you?" And don't refer to drug or alcohol abuse because you are not qualified to diagnose those problems.

- *Establish an Employee Assistance Program that aids employees in handling a wide range of personal problems as well as addictions.* From financial problems to eating disorders to alcoholism,

---

Employee Assistance Programs

What an EAP is: An EAP offers employees a confidential resource to go to when they have problems. EAPs assist employees with short-term problems, offering counseling, recommendations, referrals, and other resources to help employees get back on track if a problem is negatively affecting their lives. It is imperative that no employee ever suffer any consequences for contacting an EAP. The EAP can help a business salvage an otherwise satisfactory employee who has just experienced a setback as a result of grief, anxiety over finances, or any of a host of other personal problems.

What an EAP is not: An EAP is not a protection for an employee who is performing poorly or is being evaluated for disciplinary action. Although the employee may state that he has contacted the EAP and is optimistic about improvement, simply contacting the EAP is not a free pass to perform poorly.

How expensive is an EAP? EAPs are inexpensive and can save far more money than they cost in hiring, productivity, workers' compensation claims, and many other expenses associated with troubled employees. If a company feels that it does not have the money or time to establish its own EAP, it can share an EAP with other companies or purchase services from an outside contractor.

Employee Assistance Programs (EAPs) offer help to both employees and businesses.

- *Use state and federal resources—many of which are free—to aid you.* The Drug Free Workplace Helpline and the National Clearinghouse for Alcohol and Drug Information are two resources that can direct you to more specific information. Call your state's Department of Human Resources or visit its Web site. And you can go online and find free information on almost any specific problem, from caregiving for the elderly to pornography addiction.

EMPLOYEES WITH DRUG AND ALCOHOL PROBLEMS

Over 70 percent of all illegal drug users are employed full or part time. What does this mean to employers? The following statistics from the 'Lectric Law Library portray a sobering picture:

- One in twelve full-time employees reports currently using illicit drugs.
- One in ten people in the United States has an alcohol problem.
- Billions of dollars are lost yearly through injuries, workers' compensation claims, poor productivity, and absenteeism caused by drug and alcohol problems.

These statistics don't even begin to include employees who are addicted to prescription drugs or who fail to report problems out of fear of losing their jobs.

What are some signs that an employee may be addicted? According to DrugTestCenter.com, look for these signs:

- Changes in attendance (i.e., missing work or tardiness)
- Changes in job performance
- Changes in overall attitude or personality
- Sudden outbreaks of anger
- Changes (deterioration) in physical appearance or grooming
- Money or equipment missing from the workplace

- Complaints from coworkers or customers about the employee's attitude or behavior
- Missing work deadlines
- Shying away from responsibility

These symptoms give management a heads-up that the employee needs help. Only an attorney can advise you on what to do, but the following are some interventions to explore when dealing with this growing problem.

Interventions

- *Begin with the interventions mentioned previously in this chapter.* Most of the interventions cited were originally designed to help with drug and alcohol problems.
- *Allow employees time to participate in AA meetings, counseling, and other recovery processes.* Giving the employee time to attend meetings shows meaningful support for her recovery. These employees often feel overwhelmed; providing time helps them schedule.
- *Confidentiality is paramount.* Even if you feel that everyone knows about the employee's problem, don't mention it at work. Allow the employee to bring it up to you.
- *Document all performance problems and train your employees who supervise to do so also.* Again, you are not qualified to diagnose a drug or alcohol problem, but you can confront an employee with objective performance problems and ask if there is anything he needs in the way of help. Allow the employee to bring up drugs or alcohol; you should not.
- *Avoid including alcohol in work-related social activities or ensure sensitive handling of these events.* Do you have a keg of beer with pizza or wine with dinner? Make sure that Perrier or Calistoga Water is attractively served as well. Ideally, the behavior of non-drinking employees should be transparent to the drinkers.
- *Create balance in the workplace so that pressures do not overwhelm recovering employees and encourage them to drink.* Some work cultures are pressurized tanks of overworked people. At the end of the day, the quick route to unwinding is a drink or a drug.

Make an effort to create a workplace that allows employees time for family or recreation—within reason.

- *Drug testing is not for everyone, but it is an option that you may want to explore.* Implementing a drug testing policy should be studied carefully and with expert advice. If you do begin drug testing, be sure to spell out the consequences of positive results and apply them consistently to all employees. Advise current and prospective employees well in advance about your intention of instituting a drug testing policy.

- *Consider sponsoring support or recovery groups on site.* Although many employees will prefer the anonymity of going elsewhere, some will appreciate the convenience of having these meetings close by.

- *Offer health-care coverage that includes treatment for addiction if at all possible.* With health-care costs soaring and employers bearing the brunt of this, insurance that aids employees with addiction problems may be expensive. Before you rule it out, however, consider what impaired employees may already be costing you. In addition to all the costs already mentioned, alcoholics and other addicts have difficulty making good or timely decisions, may take longer to do assignments, and can endanger themselves and others.

EMPLOYEES WHO ARE CAREGIVERS FOR CHILDREN OR THE ELDERLY

Even if absenteeism isn't a problem, some employees bring their caregiving woes into the workplace, to the detriment of their productivity and everyone else's. Little Johnny may have chronic ear infections that the employee must discuss in minute detail with a coworker, or later Little Johnny may have frequent meetings with his parole officer for an entirely different type of chronic problem. And the National Alliance for Caregiving notes that over 22 million people are caring for elderly parents. Many problems with medical appointments, administering medication, transportation, mood swings, and financial burdens may accompany elder care.

A secondary problem is the growing resentment of employees who are not caregivers. These unfettered employees feel that they are being treated unfairly because they do not get the same breaks that the caregivers get. The resentful employees may feel that they are covering phones and services a little too often because coworkers are caring for family members.

How can your company offer a supportive environment for burdened employees while maintaining the productivity standards that the shareholders and coworkers expect? The interventions at the beginning of this chapter apply here, as do the following.

Interventions

- *Consider the support services mentioned in Chapter 7, "The Absent Employee."* On-site day care/elder care, contract services to care for sick children who can't go to school or day care, and other such services will ease the minds of distracted employees. Review that chapter for other helpful strategies.

- *In a meeting in which you express compassion, bring up written policies regarding absences or point out performance measures that indicate that the employee's performance is suffering.* Do not bring up the elderly parent or the child with needs. Discuss only the employee's performance. Be sure that all performance measures and expectations have been discussed previously or the employee may not be responsible for meeting them.

- *If the employee brings up the caregiving as a problem, brainstorm with him means of reducing the number of work hours affected by the problem.* Ask him to make a list of all the things related to the problem that are affecting his performance. After reviewing the list, offer to help him with at least one of the problems. For example, for a very valuable and deserving employee, offer a small pay raise to offset the cost of a paid caregiver. Or, you might give the employee the afternoon off to explore other care options. After you make a concession, ask the employee to put a checkmark next to any calls or activities that can be made during nonwork time. Finally, ask the employee what he thinks is fair to coworkers and to the company regarding the amount of work time he spends— *not including allowed breaks*—on personal phone calls and personal conversations. Repeat that you are supportive of his using all the break and meal time allotted to him in any way he chooses.

Express your expectation that during other work time he will concentrate on work, barring emergencies. Document this meeting, especially the part where the employee—not the employer—brought up the caregiving as a problem.

- *Remember that EAPs counsel employees about handling the problems of their children and families, not just their own problems.*
- *If the employee states that caregiving is a problem, ask her if she wants to consider a flextime arrangement.* Again, don't bring this up with the employee, but wait until the employee expresses her need for help with her caregiving problem and the impact it is having on her productivity. Explore offering flextime so that the employee is at home when a child returns from school or before the doctor's office closes. Sometimes the employee can come in early and use that extra hour or two in the afternoon to take care of responsibilities at home.

EMPLOYEES WITH FINANCIAL PROBLEMS

Financial problems can erupt in an employee's life quickly and can be as destructive as addiction or any other performance problem. Often, the employee is not to blame for the catastrophic event that put him or her in dire straits: a serious illness in the family, an accident, a lawsuit, or the needs of an elderly parent. In other cases, gambling and nonstop shopping have led the employee into financial distress. Whatever the cause, this financial predicament cannot be allowed to impair the employee's performance, or anyone else's, for the long term. Frequent calls at work from bill collectors are distracting for everyone. Receptionists may be placed in awkward situations. Some collection people may even show up on your premises. Employees may attempt to borrow from other employees, and that usually leads to disharmony. Interventions must be taken to protect the smooth operation of your organization.

Interventions

- *In general, it is wiser to pay for financial counseling for an employee who tells you that he has a problem than to give him advances or loans.* If an employee tells you that he is in financial difficulties, you may want to offer to pay for services that show him how to borrow money now but, more importantly, help avoid this situation in the future.

- *Follow the interventions mentioned earlier, particularly the ones related to EAPs.*
- *Help employees avoid this problem by offering financial counseling and programs in the workplace.* Vendors who work with your 401(k) plans or other benefits may have free speakers or videos about planning for retirement, college, or the purchase of a home. Your credit union is another source of counseling and informative programs.

EMPLOYEES WITH MENTAL ILLNESS, EMOTIONAL PROBLEMS, OR LEARNING DISORDERS

Employers are becoming more and more open to hiring employees with psychological or learning disorders for many reasons. As more people have become comfortable with seeking help for these problems and being candid about it, there are many more people in the workplace who have been treated for a short-term or chronic problem. Second, employers are realizing that many of these employees can bring great value to the workplace—if they are placed in the right position and supported. Finally, medications have made many symptoms practically a thing of the past for these challenged people.

The following interventions are possibilities as you work with these often very gifted people. Remember that these employees are probably protected by federal and state laws aimed at ensuring that employees with disabilities are supported and treated fairly. Keep that in mind and seek expert advice before implementing any intervention.

Interventions

- *If the employee has voluntarily told you of her mental, psychological, or learning disorder, ask her what she needs and wants in the way of support.* This can include a recovery partner, scheduled visits with a company nurse or psychologist, or a mentor. Be sure to get her request for one of these in writing before you proceed.

When an employee first takes a job, she is usually most willing to take measures to ensure her success. She may actually want some built-in support on the job to aid her in staying healthy. If at a later time the employee goes off her medication or demonstrates erratic behavior, her designated support system may realize the problem before she does. Again, these support systems must in no way be suggested by anyone other than the employee.

- *If you are unaware of an employee's problems until you notice behaviors on the job, use the interventions set forth at the beginning of this chapter.* Unlike some of the behaviors discussed in this chapter, however, these problems are not to be handled with disciplinary action. They are illnesses or disabilities, and employees who have them have the same legal protection as those with physical disabilities.

The problems discussed in this chapter are among the most challenging for managers and supervisors. In every case, confidentiality is imperative. On the other hand, legal and human resources professionals should be consulted to ensure that employees are treated fairly and that the company is protected from legal action. Handled correctly, employees with many of these problems can return to the workplace more productive than ever before.

Index

193

About the Author

Casey Fitts Hawley is coach and confidante to successful managers and executives at every level of corporate America. Her successful work with both gifted leaders and training executives has led to a diverse client list that includes Georgia-Pacific, Coca-Cola, Southern Company, the government of Canada, and Cox Communications. She is an executive coach to C-level clients, but she also takes joy in preparing tomorrow's leaders in various professional development programs.

She is the author of *Effective Letters for Every Occasion, 100+ Tactics for the New Office Politics,* and *100+ Winning Answers to the Toughest Interview Questions*, and is a contributor to *Chicken Soup for the Soul, III,* and various business magazines. She was awarded a National Endowment for the Humanities grant for her work in psycholinguistics and completed her postgraduate work at Stanford University.

Known for her high-energy seminars and her humorous delivery, Casey Fitts Hawley has been in demand as a speaker to *Fortune* 100 companies for over 20 years. Her Marietta, Georgia, firm offers a full range of sales and management courses in addition to team building. She also offers courses via her web site at grammarcoach.com.